PUT OUT MORE PRAYER FLAGS

By the same author:

Poetry
The Wolf Problem in Australia (1994)
Backpack Despatches: Travel Poems (1998)
The Impatient World (2002)
A Constellation of Abnormalities (2017)
Canberra Light (2019)

Chapbooks
Vanuatu Moon (vols 1 & 2; 2011 / 2012)
Greenhouse: the Penguins Revolt & Other Poems (2015)

(As compiling editor:)
Little Book of Childhood (2003)
Birds: Poems by Judith Wright (new supplemented edition, 2003)

Plays
Deadline: A Manual for Hostage-Taking
A Galah in the Samovar

Non-fiction (Compiling editor)
Acquired Tastes: Celebrating Australia's Culinary History (1998)
A Sporting Nation: Celebrating Australia's Sporting Life (1999)
The Endless Playground: Celebrating Australian Childhood (2000)

PUT OUT MORE PRAYER FLAGS

Faith, Grace, Hope, Devotion–Fragility, Responsibility–
Privilege, Relegation, Betrayal & Loss

PAUL CLIFF

RECENT
WORK
PRESS

Put Out More Prayer Flags
Recent Work Press
Canberra, Australia

ISBN: 9780645973297 (paperback)

A catalogue record for this book is available from the National Library of Australia

Cover image: Frantisek Duris via unsplash
Cover design: Recent Work Press
Set by Recent Work Press

recentworkpress.com

ss

For Skye, Hannah & Ursula

Contents

FAITH, GRACE, HOPE

CRITTERS

FOURTEEN (9 Sonnets)

TWO BUCOLICS

HISTORY & FABLES

FAITH, GRACE, HOPE

Instructions for playing piano

This instrument is to be played as if just this moment
been discovered miraculously washed up
onto the white-shingle beach of an uninhabited island
off the remote southern coast of Japan. With you tasked
with the mission of exploring the abounding mystery of it—
penetrating its occult chemistry, feeling your way in
as best you can—bit-by-bit, slow-and-steady as it goes.
Working honourably and true, in good faith,
for every millimetre of its fraught, slippery, ingenious
way—to distil its innermost essence, and pulse.
Comprehend the purity and texture of its grain,
and deep-looming, brooding possibilities of the sound
to be potentially earned from it. Testing the stresses
that can be imposed without bruising or hurt.
Eking out, via the odd, little, slow rib-poke—tweak,
tease or solicitous probe—the precise load for detonation
of each separate black and white key. Divining every
single, precious, possible note, and the laying down
of each precise, precious chord, for maximum impact—
due resonance, reverberature, nuance and frisson.
While still keeping everything simple, real, vital—
fresh, and whole.

Proceeding as if terrified this stupendous machine
might impetuously explode under your fingertips—
or that there were a finite limit to the number of notes
to be milked from it as it was 'played'—before the
little, felt-hooded hammers shrivelled and shrank
like the petals of a frost-blighted rose—the keys

irreparably warped—and catastrophically failed to
align with, and crisply strike, the precise-tensioned
spring-steel wires ... So this instrument, which had
so generously ventured to surrender and lend itself
to human hand—merely to discover the abject futility
of such—was forced to just simply give up. Allow
itself to be dragged stiff-legged off sidewards—
stone shingles clawing at its high-buffed, lacquered
sides, and scratching out the ivory whites of its eyes—
to be sucked back into the violent, black vacuity of
the sea from which it had so momentously come.
Be flipped and rolled bodily over like an end-of-life
iceberg, to implode belly-up in a cauldron of seething,
inrushing saltwater ... Sunder, break up, and die ...
Never to be remotely sighted by human eye—be heard
to sound in human ear, or felt under human hand
ever again. *Amen.*

The oar

(after Rosemary Dobson's 'The Sailor' 1960)

A sailor who had shed the sea (or perhaps
had had the sea shed him) walked far inland,
his back strapped with an Oar.
And all the way along, the people pointed at him
and guffawed—pillorying him
from their village doors. Ever ready and willing,
it seems, to show compassion, concern
and consideration for the man's Oar,
without the least being inclined to extend it to him.

Still, the man persevered. Bearing his Oar's
heavy weight with conviction, and purpose.
Persisting in calling himself a Sailor,
resolutely traipsing his way on. His Oar
growing ever more into legend—as he himself,
conversely, in the People's mind
(as if by some law of inverse proportion;
or of diminishing returns)
increasingly disappeared.

Then one day a great wave struck the coast
of that country, flooding it far inland.
When, at last, the waters receded,
a rescue party was sent out in search.
And upon its return, the People, in their ever-consuming
obsession all excitedly called:

Did you find the Oar? Did you find the Oar?
But as ever, and totally predictably, of course:
bugger-all interest or concern whatsoever
was expressed by the People for *him*.

The deep freeze (a riddle)

It is expensive to get here—and presumably likewise
to leave. A sparse population of just 55,000, spread over
an area a quarter the size of Australia. And its capital
(whose name suggests weapons of mass destruction)
is heavy with the chorus of baying huskies,
huddled in packs of up to 100 in the streets.
With one of the animals, serving as initial disruptor,
cranking the barking up for all the others to then join in.
And the streets are full of their husky shit. (Which,
peculiarly enough, on account of the piercing cold perhaps,
actually reeks less than you might expect.)

The citizens park their vehicles with their motors
left running for hours in the streets—so the engine blocks
don't freeze. And altogether it is an extreme geography:
challenging at even the most clement of times, with winter
bringing everything abjectly to its knees … So that you
wonder, in truth: Why on earth would people, in their right,
proper senses—bringing along with them the home comforts
and accoutrements of their vehicles' vulnerable engine
blocks and their packs of whining, shitting huskies,
ever volunteer to surrender themselves and come
in the first place—to live here in the Deep Freeze?

Filial: the detectives

1.
He's flying back to see his Mum in Africa.
She's got her 80th next month, and he frets for her
out there on the farm alone, in these unsettled,
post-colonial times. Though she claims in fact
she's right as rain—with the farm manager living
nearby; and his sister making the two-hour
drive from Port Elizabeth to stay weekends
sometimes. And her gardening and pottery class
to keep her occupied. In addition to her traditional
and ritual pastime of reading detective novels in the bath.
Lolling there for hours at a stretch, soaking up
the hard-boiled classics: Hammett, Chandler, Runyon,
Spillane. And her favourite, Georges Simenon.

2.
He's flying back to see his Mum in Africa.
He's made it every second year of the past 12.
She'd had him late: at 45, and contrary to medical
advice. She wasn't fazed—and both came through
it fine; to form a special bond perhaps. So to see her in
her present plight, at this late juncture of her life,
just isn't right. It can't be healthy for her there, out on
her own so far from town, with just the manager nearby.
And that motley detective gang of the pulp-fiction kind
for closer company. Cavorting there bathside,
messing with her poor, tired heart and mind
in the late afternoon, or evening time. (And especially,
from what he's heard, that Belgian letch, Georges Simenon.)

3.

He's flying back to see his Mum in Africa,
to celebrate her 80th next month. And have
a good stern talk with her. If he can just wrangle
some quality talk-time away from those detectives
forever crowding her. As she lolls there in the bath,
and in suspended time, throughout the long late
afternoons, and on into the evenings. It used to
drive his poor dad nuts, her hogging the bathroom
like that—in such shameless and brazen consort
with those sordid private Dicks.
And, with all the down-time that's been available
in these six years since his father's passed,
her detective habit's just grown worse. Yes, there's
no holding that woman down, if there's a tub of good
hot soapy water and some dependable crime fiction
lying round. High time for him to fly out there
and sort the matter out.

4.

High time for him to fly out there, and sort her
living choice. Residing there alone, barricaded
in behind the bathroom door for these past 15 years
or more, with those disreputable detectives
huddled in close round. He must admit, it's amusing
though, to imagine her in there with them.
Holding court in all that steam with Hammett, Chandler
and Runyon—Spillane and Simenon. The stinking fug
of cheap stogie cigars; and the language getting pretty
blue you'd think, at times. The soft chinkling of shots
of rye, nudged slyly into tumblers from the bottle
in the vanity's bottom drawer. And the men got up

a poker game or maybe playing pinochle: condensation
beading on their brows and shoulder-holstered .45s.
With her gentle laugh—or her loose cough—sidling
from beneath the door. Or her solitary murmuring:
as she's heard to softly interrogate herself sometimes—
So you're not sure whether to smile or feel concerned.

5.

Yes, well: whether he should laugh or feel concerned,
he's flying out next week in any case. She's shrinking
right away he swears: got smaller each occasion
that he's seen her, these last few recent times. It's got to
be that tub-soaking, and bad influence of those damned
detectives. High time to take the matter firm in hand:
get her to sell up the farm, and move into his sister's
place in Port Elizabeth. It's only right he tries to help,
at this stage of her life—after all the woman's done
for him—right from the start, commencing with the
very act of giving birth to him. (Her 'bright-eyed golden
boy', so-called.) To not act now would be completely
unforgivable—criminal, almost. It's more than time
to wean the woman off those pulp detectives now …
So anyway, that's the plan: to jump aboard that plane,
and fly straight there next week. Time's truly come
to finally sort this whole despicable mess of her
and that entire gang of degenerate detectives out.

Put out more prayer-flags: a vernacular lay

1. Purchase ('Made to fade')

(Bus Depot Markets, Kingston)

The prayer-flags retail in two kinds: traditional
Kathmandu imports, poorly printed upon thin cloth—
and stouter-stitched, industrial-strength types,
stamped with heavy black lettering and manufactured
here. The first last two years; the second for five
(approx). Still, you opt for the former: obsolescence
precisely being the point. These flags are made to fade—
for their bright-coloured bunting to be chewed
to diaphanous rags. Eaten alive by wind, sun,
rain and frost—frayed and flayed sheerer than
negligée. Buddha scalded-and-blanched, as they
trip their way gloriously onward and outward,
leaching back to the pure, blue-gold breast of God.

2. Stringing them up in the Manchurian pear

To trip their way back to the blue Godhead,
you string the flags up in your yard—staggering in
artful, zigzag array, up through the tabby-barked
limbs of the Manchurian pear. Stepping-stones
of bright-brazen cloth, strung whimsically
every-whichway: like crosspatch lightning,
or some looney-tunes ship's swashbuckling rigging.
Gaudy as a blitzed paintbox, or some Deity's

aniline-dyed handkerchiefs. Hitching their
bareback ride on the Sky's wind-horse, for their
printed word-cargo to continually peel off and be
borne helter-skelter away. Running themselves
ragged in their persistent, perpetual, pliant pilgrimage
and hallowed crepitation. Fluttering, flattering
and dancing their way toward Grace.

3. Fighting this good, fair, gentle jihad

The flags flutter and flatter their Grace-ward way
in persistent, pliant pilgrimage. Though in fact,
you're embarrassed to say, you haven't a clue what
the Sanskrit script might actually denote. Specifically;
in so many words. But their intent would be worthy,
you're sure. The flags seem good-natured and true,
personable and purposeful enough—brandishing
themselves in bravura display, dancing their pretty way
branch-to-branch. Their message would be cogent
and sensible, you'd hope—you're happy to take
the matter on trust, anyway: to give them their head—
full rein and sway to tout themselves, as they
mingle and banter on the tree's backstairs.
Broadcasting their cheery whatever-message
aloft—making their lackadaisical way from your
backyard out into the wider World. As all the while
their bunting gradually fritters, frays and wanes
in the task. Fighting this goodly, gentle, protracted—
joyous and glorious jihad.

4. Good, gentle soldiers and willing slave-workers

Fighting their gentle and joyous jihad, these flags
are Hope's stalwarts—warriors and diehards.
A praetorian guard, fighting from the pear's stronghold.
Pledged to serving and protecting your house, in this
frantic, teeming, ever-teetering World. Soldier-workers
in the great, thrumming blue-&-white hive of this
bitter-sweet, spinning Earth. With Faith's workhorse-wind
riding them hard—treadmilling the stencilled words in
their cloth to keep the prayers lean and clean; trim, taut
and terrific. A vital chain-gang of Trust, exhausting itself
in thrall to the overseer Sky: harnessed to its vast, infinite,
intricate, blue treadwheel. Ever-willing slave-workers
in Time's great Universal gulag.

5. The flags grow gradually weary and blistered all over

Ever-willing slave-workers in Time's gulag,
the flags boldly treadmill the air from the pear
in your yard. Their bright-coloured cloth unflaggingly toils,
as they ply their prayer-muscle in incessant labour.
Grow gradually weary, wear themselves down—
falter, fade, fray and abrade. Bleach, blench and blanch.
Pray till their lips are blistered all over: till their cloth
is tattered and sore, and they can pray not a single
prayer-syllable more—but stagger and droop
and cling bruised to their rope. The Sky drained
and honed them—filleted and boned them to pure,
pale, raggedy filigree. Worked them till all of their
valiant goodwill's been transmitted—transmuted.

Till they've utterly expended themselves, and have got
nothing more—their message broadcast to the point
of obliteration, almost. And their once bright-brazen,
heaving prayer-ship has gone down by the bow.

6. 'Your Message has been sent'

(Or: 'Hey Dad, the prayers are all gone now!')

Their great-heaving prayer-ship goes down by the bow,
its bright-stencilled messages fully expired. And, for all
of their valiant and heroic service, it's admittedly true
that towards their end now, the flags are hardly a pretty
sight. Limp, peeling, scabrous, tatty discards; bedraggled,
torn, forlorn and discordant. Gibbeted, palely flapping there,
set against the Manchurian's new bloom—with the look
of old dishcloths; of the foot-rags of some routed Grand Armée,
unpicked and cast to roadside; or the desiccated hides of
wasted carcasses hung on the dog tree, to stiffly twist in the breeze.
So that your daughter is prompted to point at the pear, and ask:
'Hey Dad, the prayers are all gone now. They've been
sent to God. Can we take the prayer-flags down now, pu-*lease*!'

7. Taking the broken prayers down

Yes, well: the prayers are all gone. 'Been sent to God,
now', as your daughter tells. (You suppose.) And, duly
chastised, and just as instructed, you untie the flags' cord
from the Manchurian's branches. Snatch, tug, yank
and wrangle: slowly dismantle the things by the fistful,
in great metre-length hanks—till the pear stands scalped

of its artful prayers, and you clutch their limp mess
in a ropey tangle, like a brace of slain gamebirds
dangling in both hands ... To now ponder the proper,
most appropriate means to dispose of them. Bin them?
Burn—or cremate—them? Toss them into the compost,
to break down, recycle and reincarnate? What's the Godhead's
preference, pray? Then, taking a wider look around, you realise
how, without the flags' presence, the tree, yard, house
and everything else seem to suddenly shrink and cower.
Loom dangerously vulnerable and imperilled, somehow.

8. A brief interregnum

Yes, without the flags' big-shouldering, free-skipping,
presence, everything seems to shrink and cower.
Appear suddenly stricken and bereft—eerily and alarmingly
exposed, somehow. The Manchurian standing brutally
stripped, in the shocking regime of its new prayerless state:
marooned under the baleful weight of the untamed Sky.
As, over subsequent days meanwhile, in the absence
of the tree's happy, habitual, go-to talismans,
the household chips in with cheery suggestions for dressing
the pear anew: Try flying or hanging something else up there
in the prayer-flags' lieu—like a hammock, a birdfeeder,
or a windchime, say. Or a Chippewa Nation dream-catcher
maybe (which prayer-flags, sort of, essentially are in a way,
it could be argued?) But you're personally unconvinced.
With things in this World being as continually ornery,
complex and uncertain as they are, and potential peril
lurking everywhere, in manifold and infinite ways—
ever *more* recourse ought to be made to prayer-flags,

you reckon—and urgently, too. Yes, for sure: to replenish
the tree with fresh prayers is far and away the very best move.

9. Resurgence: prayer-flags redux

Yes, to refurbish the tree with prayer-flags is the sanest
thing to do. I'm feeling it, I really am. To recharge the
household, and reconstitute matters: make everything vital
and whole. And a fortnight later, sure enough, a skein of
brand-spanking new flags is there. Resumed their tenure:
ripely unfurled and flying high, fecund with fresh-minted prayer.
The tree juddering and rollicking with new prayer-fruit.
The Sky's wind-horse set their cloth at full canter, in a big-bright,
lairy, Zorro-like covenant zigzagging the pear tree's branches.
Hope's big-humming, tremoring, red, yellow, green, white
and blue ensign set skating and skiddering in the breeze.
Our household put safely back under the flags' purview,
and receiving due blessing again. (If admittedly with a
hammock concessionally slung up there, along with them
in the Manchurian too.)

The prayers recommenced their marathon trek, and kindly,
patient onslaught to providential dissolution. And set to fly
there for a good many more seasons yet, if I've any fair say
in it. Yes: Prayer-flags doing frank-and-fearless service,
fiercely plying the wild, woolly blue forever, is my fervent
pledge, and ardent conviction. My inviolable point of view.

Prescription for joy and peace in this world (a rave)

IF: Russia could just sit back, content to rest on its laurels, confident in already possessing the largest national landmass in the world—9000 kilometres in length, stretching from Kaliningrad Oblast on the Baltic, all the way east to Cape Dezhnev in the Bering Strait—*AND* could shrug off its onerous, centuries-long, baked-in tradition of strongman-despotism, to indulge its more feminine side and embrace a liberal Europe—*AND*: If Putin and his oligarch mates could return (ooh say) just 9/10 of the national wealth that they've plundered and squirrelled away for themselves (still leaving the President enough in his pocket to buy up half of the Cote d'Azur to retire to and pose there bare-chested astride his white horse, flexing his pecs for the next cover-shot of *Field & Stream, Fortune* or *Vanity Fair*)—*THEN*, well: America could be given the smart smack on its nose which it so richly deserves and desperately needs, and be told to get back in its box, give itself a good general makeover, and clean up its own nest of longstanding, niggling concerns—like its race problem, mass school shootings, widespread inequities of wealth, and the pernicious, underlying malaise of its military-industrial complex cum perpetual war economy—and could man itself up to the truth-telling of Julian Assange, rein in Big Tech and Big Pharma, and future-proof itself against rabid demagogic disruptors like Trump—to thus nudge its way somewhere nearer to becoming the big, bright-shiny Jeffersonian ideal from which it's allegedly sprung (and which, in its insistent PR, it incessantly cracks itself up to be) … So, well, *THEN*: the whole World could breathe easier! And, in between binging itself sick on Netflix and shopping till it drops in the gleaming pox of its vast and resplendent hypermalls, find time to belatedly finetune its plans to lower its Greenhouse emissions … Could relax, chill—and just *hang*. While saving its real energy and strength, of course, for the big looming headache of CHINA—shadow-boxing in the hall up the way.

Skyfall

Things officially attested as having fallen
from the sky include:

> wool thread, and candy,
> winkles, worms, snakes,
> frogs and toads,
> varieties of beans and grains,
> blood, meat, muscle and fat,
> lizards, lichen, eels;
> fish species of multifarious kinds
> (catfish, trout, herring,
> sardines, perch and suchlike) …
> Something described as 'angel hair'?
> Glowing jelly and green peaches,
> flocks of birds—and banknotes.

Plus, a carpenter working on a roof
was impaled by a two-metre shaft of ice,
one time.

There's also meteors (or 'shooting stars').
And, too obvious to mention, Sun and Rain, of course.
And, fading in and out of this,
those usual recalcitrants: the UFOs.
God. And Hope.

The waiting: the hospice, the fisherman

1. The hospice

The view to die for gives through a double-glazed
window, out onto a lake of wraparound water
in a 270-degree wheel. So the place feels like an island,
almost. Honey-lit poplars spiral up into the glittering
autumn air, their dropped leaves a sodden porridge
of yellow oatmeal or kind of thick, vegetably soup.
Bare willows are weeping bankside—where a pair of
contractors are on their knees, extending a flowerbed wall.

Inside, all seems precision-designed for dignity, calm
and respect. A restrained décor of pastel tones, TV sets
discreetly tumbling online video. Some rooms have
an overnight visitor's bed—and all in all it feels like some
weirdly exclusive motel. In which the residents just lie back,
relax, and leisurely cruise—as the big picture-window
meanwhile erupts with the urgent, rude life outside,
crashing past, head-over-heel.

> Hunched rollerbladers sawing by,
> knees and elbows padded up to prevent hurting
> themselves; a yummy-mummy in tiger-pattern
> leotards, jogging a 3-wheeler pram
> to chase down her pre-pregnancy shape;
> power-walkers, out striving for their rightful,
> due powerful health.

There's always something worth happening here
at this stretch of the lake, and on the abutting cycle path.

And the sunny courtyard where we sit with her now
is alive with birds: robins, blue wrens, wagtails.
And a magpie, which one of the residents feeds Cheezels
to—despite repeated scolding by nursing staff, our friend tells.
'Apparently Cheezels aren't good for the magpies' health,'
she gently laughs, head tilted back in its pale-blue
headscarf. Still, they can't seem to stop the woman from
doing it. In face of Life's brazen intransigence,
there are limits to what you can do.

2. The fisherman

Drinking a beer with her husband on his verandah
that afternoon, it's clear he's recently lost some
weight too. As if Death's taking them in a package deal.
Unshaven jaw. Thousand-yard stare, like a soldier requiring
urgent withdrawal from the field—his eyes boring holes
into the chaos of spilt compost and straw of the abandoned
herb bed he's half built.

And there are kids tangled up in all this mess too.
The eldest is faring as well as you could expect,
with support of her friends and school, he tells—
but the boy has completely shut down: fallen into
the electric black hole of his PlayStation. Bunkered
down deep in his bedroom.

> 'Big thumbs kids have these days,' he nods,
> raising his boxer's hands to wriggle his own,
> and mime the gaming moves.
> 'I keep telling him he's got to start to dealing with it,
> and soon—It's time.'

Then, as he takes another slow pull on his beer, I ask:
'And how about you?'
A moment's weary consideration, before that
battlefield stare again.

> 'Sometimes I'm okay with it. Really.
> I can accept it almost, you know.
> Other times, I think that this world's
> one dark, twisted, fucked-up place.
> Throwing stuff like this in your face—
> and especially at kids …
>
> But *mainly* now, I just look on it as a *job*.
> Which I have to get us all through.
> It's taking so long, and I feel so consumed—
> but one day pretty soon the thing will be done.
> We'll be there. And I'll have space
> to think about something else.'

Arching one wild-looking brow, he glances up
at the 12-foot beach rod he's set hanging between
the veranda posts. Scratches his jaw, then nods:
> 'And maybe I can get back down to the coast again
> for a bit of fishing, too.'

CRITTERS

Crocodiles: the Far North

(Or: Ten ways of looking at a crocodile)

1.

Cairns Post, Wednesday 13 July: Two Crocodiles were placed on good behaviour bonds at the Court of Petty Sessions here today, after uttering menaces to a Danish tourist at a popular Daintree swimming hole.

2.

A local tells that he once saw a man stood waist-high in a creek by his boat, with his two kiddies wading thigh-high nearby, in full view of a Crocodile warning-sign—as a Croc worked its way round his boat's other side. 'Bloody tourists you get up here!' he snorts: 'Total *fucking* idiots eh!'

3.

The cane-train driver strolling Cardwell Beach keeps five metres clear of the water's edge: just beyond reach of what a Croc could competently hurl itself, he reckons. But admits that he *does* sometimes worry about the reckless plashing of his unleashed dog.

4.

First time out fishing since moving up North, the Sydney man reports to his wife that he needs to buy a bigger boat—or one bigger, say, than the biggest known local Croc, at least.

5.

The reason for so few published reminiscences of growing up in the Far North, is that so few of the people who grow up here survive Crocodile attacks in their childhoods.

6.

Crocodiles and the Yeppoon Paradise Resort negotiate a *quid pro quo*:
Resort guests won't trespass in the Crocodile's ocean, if the Croc keeps
its big nasty, gnarly snout right out of the guests' infinity pool.

7.

The woman serving us breakfast at the Babinda Café tells that the local
Croc (name of 'Clyde') can be seen sunning himself on the riverbank
by the bridge, just a kay out of town, on any normal workday. And
when we go for a look, sure enough Clive's lolled there—relaxed,
and amiable enough. Smiling with the crinkly, roué-like charm of a
late-career Maurice Chevalier. (Warbling 'Thank Heaven for Little
Girls', in that grainy-grey youtube-clip footage of the *Royal Variety
Command Performance* of 1959.)

8.

Just for a moment, try imagining *this* story line: 'Yesterday morning
a man was taken at a popular fishing spot by a three-and-a-half metre
Dugong. Police and Park Rangers are tracking the animal down, with
hope of retrieving the man's remains.'

Doesn't work—*Right?* The animal lacks the requisite gravitas, and
credible capacity for savage, unleashed aggression. To pull *that* kind of
story off, you need something way higher up the food chain—an apex
predator, like a Croc.

9.

'Just because you can't see a Crocodile, don't think one's not watching
you,' our river-tour operator warns. From mangroves, beaches and
creeks running all the way down Australia's east coast from the tip
of Carpentaria to just below Gympie, evidently, these days—with
maverick sightings as far south as Stradbroke. At which point,

for whatever wily, antediluvian contrivances of its own, the Croc presence abruptly stops: so it's just the Great Whites and the Irukandji that you need to worry about, on entering the water again.

10.

News report, Cairns Post, Friday September 21: Last night two Crocodiles serving good behaviour bonds carjacked a grey-nomad couple's Winnebago from outside the Cane Cutter Hotel and ramraided the Mossman IGA. After making off with a dozen size-16 frozen chickens and a 500-pack carton of Benson & Hedges, they were stopped at a police roadblock on the Kuranda road, and are currently held on remand pending appearance in Atherton County Court.

Crocodile: a re-evaluation

(What the Croc really wants)

Despite its undoubted 'formidable' reputation,
university research has consistently shown
that what every Crocodile fundamentally wants,
like any of us, is some respite from the chill
winds of this World. The chance to feel cherished,
and receive routine tokens of endearment and affection;
its fair quantum of hugs, kisses and cuddles.
To be succoured, and nurtured—to fulfil its personal
and professional ambitions, be revealed to its most
advantaged light, and reach its best, potential Crocodile-self.
In short: to achieve its rightful, due 'Destiny', in accordance
with its noble birthright, and its venerable lineage
as 'sacred creature' as underwritten by half the mythologies
of this world. To be—just as the Ancient Egyptians had it,
and the contemporary Melanesians probably still do—
both *'Feared and Revered'*. As the epithet goes.
To be accepted—as naturally as the lightning which brazenly
staggers about in the overhead skies—as an essential, vital,
cyclic, replenishing force, and inalienable part of the
reinvigorative, cleansing flux and thrust of this Earth.

Yes, under that big lunkhead's awry, hyper-incisored
dentury an oceanic repository of tenderness lies.
Like dry spinifex cupped in some sage elder's hands,
tremoring for its spawn-spark to be breathed upon …
for the flame to ignite—catch, hatch and spread.
Come sidling its way up from the animal's great-wrinkled
heart, rampaging out through its crinkly-thick,

prehistoric hide—to temper the sides of its antediluvian
mouth to a smile, and set light glowing in its beautiful,
freckled, mustard-gold eyes ... as the creature stands tall,
enfolded in the great-knobbly, throbbing cloak of all
its innate compassion and warmth, eager to play some
benevolent part in the mechanics of this rude world.
(Inasmuch, at least, as the treacherous regime of our
contemporary, WOKE-buggered 'Cancel-Culture' allows.)

So—When you next hear that admittedly initially dubious
if not plain outright scary '*heavy slosh*' sound: intimating
the fevered scampering of something pretty momentous,
claw-footed and substantially fixated, launching itself
from the mangrove bank: don't panic and automatically
presume its intentions malign. That the thing's necessarily
going balls-out, got some raging hard-on, to get at you ...

Though, that said, the possibility is *there*, of course.
Imprisoned in the dark web of its own involuntary instincts—
under crushing weight of inherent internal pressure—
millennial-old patterns of behaviour can be hard to break.
Some baser impulse beyond the animal's reasonable capacity
to control might be triggered—to come crawling out of the
genetic woodwork (or '*woodpile*'?). The creature might suffer
some occasional ill-judgment—be induced by pure, opportunistic
instinct, or simple Pavlovian response, into acting against
the 'Angel of its Better Nature'. Just as much as any of us.
It's certainly within its evolutionary purview to succumb
to intemperate behaviour. The animal is as fragile—as
susceptible to upwelling insecurities, doubts or conflicted emotions—
as any other sentient creature of this world. Might be excused
for growing overenthused or overplayful as, say, any large

household dog; and for committing some occasional, unseemly
impropriety or more brazen outright violation of your private
person or the private person of somebody else. May blindly
lash out to savage, or maul you. Sweep you up in some kind
of 'death-roll' or what-have-you—and drag you beneath the sweet,
chocolate-hued waters.

It'd be naive to rule the possibility *entirely* out:
It's only human, after all.

'The Roots of Heaven' (Elephant speaks)

(Film, 1958, dir John Huston, prod Darryl F Zanuck)

Like so many of Humanity's productions,
it was compromised from the start. Hampered by
protracted script rewrites, and the participants' various
inadequacies and emotions—jealousy, lust, loneliness,
self-doubt—throughout the long, arduous shoot. As well
as by the trials and exigencies of French Equatorial Africa
itself: with the sun melting the actors' makeup; cast and
crew suffering heatstroke, amoebic dysentery and malaria.
Trevor Howard (as 'crusading environmentalist', Morel)
seemed profoundly depressed, blasting himself on scotch
in his tent, all the while when off-set. Eddie Albert (as
photojournalist, Abe Fields) badly pined for his wife back home.
Zanuck—who, believe it or not, would later express his regret at
being unable to film live footage of the shooting of a real herd of
elephants for the project: feeling constrained by 'all the
humanitarian hooey' which the act would generate—was
tormented by his fruitless pursuit of gorgeous but aloof Juliette
Greco (playing Minna—nightclub hostess cum prostitute).
While Errol Flynn (as alcoholic veteran Major Forsythe,
attempting to redeem himself from some past wartime disgrace)—
and who would, by eponymous reputation, and back in his salad
days, have been 'in like Flynn' *himself* with Juliette, fair bet
(and maybe even still got there as things were, who knows?)
—was exhausted, pasty-looking, and less than a year from death.
John Huston, the film's Director (who was seemingly
obtuse, like Zanuck, to the film's underlying spirit or message)
kept the back of his Land Rover stacked with hunting guns
and ammunition in hope of slinking off to bag a trophy elephant

head, following disappointment from a failed safari
during filming of *The African Queen* three years earlier—
made the best fist of the film that he could. But would later
confess to his biographer that the depths of Romain Gary's
novel were ultimately left sadly untouched: 'It could have been
a fine picture but unfortunately wasn't.'

And as for we Elephants: Well, after the set-piece scene where
the oddbod band of lumpen do-gooders storms the hunting club
at gunpoint, for Peer Qvist to lay Madame Orsini across his lap
and ruche her hunting-skirt up to give her buttocks a round spank
of profound reprimand on Our behalf—we nodded due thanks,
wryly winked, and then, like the good, stolid, patient and
decent World creature-citizens we are—sidled off in our
lumbering, high-shouldered, sway-gaited, saggy-arse
way. Traipsing off from the whole tawdry scene—back out
into the infinite horizon and timeless dust of Mother Africa.
Thinking quietly to ourselves:

> 'Cripes, the Human Beings of this World! It seems
> that everything beautiful in it is doomed to go.
> One day these fools will be left all alone in this Earth's
> mirey wallow, with nothing to do but get themselves
> drunk, hunt, slash each other's throats and chase each
> other's tails for another quick, frantic hump. Till eventually
> they've all destroyed themselves ... Just watch!'

Sea eagle

(New Year's Day, Quaama)

Your nest is a slovenly, couch-sized construct,
staggering in its rudeness and power.
A Kontiki of sticks swept up by the vortex
of a waterspout into the fork of a towering gum.
And, more staggering still, is the sight of you,
leaning out from it—then pushing with great white-socked
feet, to drop and momently impale yourself on air.
Before idly regathering, to swoop long, steady and slow,
keeping limber and loose—
wheeling away in the direction of the sea.

Your heart equal in size to that which beats
in the chest of the child who now bends to retrieve
a speckled tailfeather from the ferns below.
Raises it overhead, and smiles—
then jiggles its quill-point against the wash
of the blue, light-blasted sky.

Wildlife

(Dunbogan, mid north coast, New South Wales)

Wildlife is profligate here; the place simply
haemorrhages it. A goanna, like a whippet on broken legs,
bails us up on the garden path. A tree snake does its
slick, zig-zag breakdance—
       one lightning-quick whipcrack down through the feijoa
         into the grass and it's gone!
A lone, scouting sea eagle slides the sky
like an ice-hockey puck,
as you watch in your bathrobe from the bedroom window.
Wattlebirds chortle all day long, nosing the fat-coned banksias.
Black cockatoos squawk out on their dawn patrol,
then reel drunkenly back homeward over the dusk mangroves.
Sugar gliders clamber next doors' TV aerial
for their evening base-jump: scooting across wide-armed
in their wing-suits, to latch onto the trunk of our blueberry ash.

And, while strolling North Beach this afternoon,
those six glossy, soot-coloured dolphins:
caught in the high-rolling shoulder
of a wave's tottering showcase.
Giddying to watch: just six metres out there,
and keeping pace abreast.

      As if I was walking them on a leash—
      or was it *them* that were walking me?

Whippet

A whippet is as close as you can conscionably get
to having a dog without having one: a tripping cloud
on velvet pads; a jonquil bouquet on clittering claws—
wrapped up in the clean, vital essence of itself ...
the merest, peripheral whiff,
and slenderest canine *intimation*. A dog-phantom:
winsome, demure, finetuned and air-filled (possibly confected
from fairy-floss).

It is all lean waist, and savagely concave belly,
skulking haunch and arced backbone—
trotting equably, tip-tripping its crimpish way along,
with nose held steadfastly down to the ground.
And the sense of having suffered some past trauma—
intemperate chastening, outright beration,
or otherwise having sound reason to feel unsure
or ashamed of itself from something back
in its unfortunate or scurrilous doggy past.

Its stance is tentative; or equivocal. Its shoulders
and flanks tremoring as if with Parkinsons—
from effort of containing the sheer vitality
of itself. As if just exploded from the sprinting-block
to instantaneously achieve top speed—then need
to sharply rein itself in and sit pat on a steady jog.
So as not to alarm the smug burghers of poor,
shockable, speed-fearing Tidy-Town
with sight of its naked, precipitative rapacity.
And so draw unwelcome attention to itself.

It is a cross between a dog and a kangaroo—
or the closest that a dog could ever evolve
toward becoming a swan. And, as your forefinger
traces along under its gracile, marsupial-like
jaw—or your hand cradles its fine, fragile
marsupial skull—likewise feels capable of sustaining itself
just by eating grass.

It is a creature of spare, delicately architected beauty.
Its elite-athleticism ringing out through the consummate
engineering of every subtle, propelling muscle,
and signified by its limber track-&-field gait,
as it hovers there, light-boned, suspended in air
a few millimetres above the ground. Its skin
glowing with the subtle, internal incandescence
of a Danish designer-light, set artfully and companionably
low over a dining table.

It is a trembling lamp-wick, set on curved hockey-stick
legs—and could light your way through the vale
of this oafish world. If you'd license it to; and concede
to follow. Though you'd need to keep wary eye too,
that the thing didn't suddenly grow weary, or bored,
with great-lumbering you—take a quick, wilful sidestep
to evanesce. Atomise itself. Disappear clear from view:
leaving you gasping and flailing there, oxygen snatched
from right out of your lungs, as it blithely floats on.
With delicate, teasing flicks of its slender, knowing
whippet-hips. And dipping nods of its long, whippish tail,
sweeping down to modestly seclude its slick tidy, prim,
butter-clean whippet-arse… Ghosting its way
off upon mouse-quiet claws—sliding on silver castor-paws.

Absolved itself utterly of you and your cause in this world,
to leave you exiled: as it proceeds somewhere thither unseen,
and aeons ahead.

Intractable and unentreatable as a collapsing
white dwarf, or a full-blown black hole. Sucked all
the vital essence from you—just catastrophically gone.

The tiger quoll coat

(For Oong)

First—find your Quoll. Being aware, however,
that as a native species this animal is strictly
protected. So, barring being sneaky and going rogue,
you'll need to luck out and find one lying dead
at the side of the road. If so: sling the thing into your
car-boot. Bring it home, skin it, and tan the hide—
then you're set to make a coat of it, to suit up the family dog.

If your dog should baulk at wearing it,
and resist being coaxed or cajoled,
try lining the hide with an old woollen vest
(Vinnies and The Salvos are good sources for this)—
attach a belly-strap fitted with buttons or Velcro,
to ensure a secure and comfortable fit—
and your dog will hopefully soon settle down,
adjusting amicably into it.

Meanwhile of course, you'll want to retain
the Quoll's interesting bones. (Or certainly the pretty
skull, at least.) So, keeping the bagged carcass on hold
in your kitchen freezer, research the most practicable
immediate means of removing the flesh from it.
　　(Burial, and decomposition—in real-time,
　　or perhaps accelerated by lime? Placing it on
　　an ants' nest? Some alternative chemical means?...)

Finally, at the end of which, two essential questions are posed:

1. As you observe your dog swanning around the house,
   flaunting its new-fangled coat: Is it the Dog's spirit
   that you see, trotting companionably along inside
   the Tiger Quoll? Or the *Tiger Quoll*'s spirit
   holding out in there, stalking maverick and wild within *it*?

And:

2. When the time comes (as it unfortunately
   but equably must) to skin the Dog:
   What animal will be privileged
   with wearing the pelt-coat
   derived from your skinning of *it*?

In sum: There are multifarious tracks in this Universe
which a Tiger Quoll and a domestic dog
might go sniffing their separate ways down.
And suiting your dog up in the *couture*
of a well-crafted coat, sourced from the end-of-life
stage of a Tiger Quoll—as opposed to one sourced from
some vulgar, *'arriviste'* exotic—like a rabbit,
a camel—a cat, donkey, fox or mink—
is as good as any way to proceed, perhaps.
Or something which you might take time
to potentially profitably consider, at least.

Privilege: the crooked white pekin

(Geehi Flats campground)

Lifting the duck from the river,
he commences carefully towelling it.
It's named 'Stargazer', he says:
on account of being born with an up-twisted neck
caused by Vitamin-B deficiency while in the egg.

Berocca had helped with the neck-straightening,
but was too late for the in-turned right leg.
The other ducks gang up on it—and would kill it
if left home alone in the yard.
So it accompanies them when they travel,
riding a pillow set between them
on their campervan's front seat

'It's like something out of Leunig,' my wife says,
as the man moves off: walking tall
and straight-backed as the fourth Magi,
his bird-gift cradled in arm—
and with no sense of irony at all,
in his telling any of this.
        If you happen to have a special-needs duck,
        this is simply the way you parent it.

And the duck, for its part, rides high and dry,
steady and calm—enfolded in its fluffy white towel.
As if such care and devotion were its simple and natural due,
and no more than what all the World's halt, lame,
crooked creatures had every right to expect.

Shark: 'bite'

The word 'Bite' seems woefully insufficient—
naff, and pedestrian—to denote the real scale
and trauma of the event. (More apt for signifying
a wound inflicted by a possum or dog.) 'Maul' works,
sort of—if more true to the manner and style of a lion
taking down a gazelle at some Serengeti waterhole;
with its trailing adjunct of the prey being dragged
bodily off, for casual ongoing 'mauling' nearby.
'Savage', too, isn't quite up to the job: seeming
inappropriately judgemental and wilfully anthropocentric,
for describing what is simply the quite natural—'proper
and proportionate' (*animal*) response of a *wild creature*,
after all … Though it certainly serves better than 'Eat',
'Taste', 'Lick'— 'Macerate', 'Masticate', and their ilk;
which are all equally, inordinately lame. And so just leaves
recourse to clichéd 'Attack'—with its unhappy sense
of whooping Apaches with tomahawks raised,
falling on the hapless wagon train. Or screaming Stukas
raining hellfire down on horse-backed Polish cavalry.

Could shanghaiing a word from some other culture's
vocabulary help? Pillage something from the Magyars
or Zulus, say? (Or more likely, I suppose, given their
marine environs, some *Pacificker* type's word-hoard.)
Or alternatively again, cutting straight to the chase,
could we forge some bespoke word of our own?:
Does some *neologism* call? The Dictionary's always got
its ear pressed to the ground, eager for the sound of
some useful, new-toddling word's footfall.
(Suggestions, anyone?)

In any case, in face of our patent etymological destitution,
until some working solution comes, and we've managed
to fill this onerous philological hole with something more
eminently sensible and suitable in our own home tongue ...
And in the abject absence of some handy, multi-tooled
('all-terrain') device, like the Inuit's 22 different words
for 'snow' (or actually, is it for 'ice'?:

>eg: 'sea'-type versus 'freshwater'; the stuff that
>you sink into up to your knees; the kind which rimes
>your SUV's side-window; or that you saw through
>to harvest as building blocks to construct your igloo,
>*Etcetera*)—

we're lexically snookered, it seems. And so, though the word
falls dismally short—and is plain utterly ludicrous for expressing
the degree of offence, and the depth of grievous physical and/or
psychological harm and hurt incurred—the word 'Bite' (or 'Bitten')
will have to suffice. For the present, 'Bite's' pale stop-gap
just has to do.

Two songs for porcines

1. The pig: a defence

Pigs cop their fair share of abuse—snide sidewards
remarks and oblique slurs. Subtle and less-subtle
forms of vilification or contumely—in metaphors
reaching deep down into the dark-bruised bones
of multiple languages and cultures of this world.
      'Fat as a—', 'eat'/'sweat'/'act'/'stink like a—'
      'Pearls before swine'. 'Lipstick on a—',
      'Hey get off the bloody couch you *porker!*'…
      (Even 'pig in a poke' and 'pork-barrelling'
      may essentially be ungenerous, or disingenuous,
      in their spirit too?) …
Ramping all the way up to the Biblical-grade curse
used to nuke the Gadarenian swine, and send them
crashing head-over-hocks, demon-clogged to their eyeballs,
into the river to be drowned.

Yet, along with dolphins, squid, octopi and apes,
they are among the most evolved of this earth's
creatures, we are told. Companionable, intelligent
and affectionate as a dog—if allowed. (And less finicky
too, you'd think, with their food.)

High time then to give them their rightful pig-place,
and meet-and-proper porcine due. Show some
inter-special respect—the maturity and moral backbone
to tear the whole despicable Pig paradigm down
and construct things more equably anew … If not

quite going so far as to conceive the pig '*hip*', then kick
things a little way down along the road at least.
Beyond the snuffling-snorting caricature which
commodifies the thing as curlicue-tailed delicatessenry—
a trooping package of bacon rashes and sausages,
stumping its way through this world upon four cloven
feet, and a thick-set back pair of smoked or honey-glazed
hams. Yes: time to see the beast for the whole vital, seething,
oxygen-breathing, milk-suckling, sentient and kindred
mammalian creature that it is. And to which it has every
inherent evolutionary right to lay claim … If not actually
a case of '*Pigs Rule Okay!*', then at least give the animal
a ticket to pass as a somewhat 'less-equal'-niche citizen
than us. Could we say?

2. Pigs don't fly (a backstory)

Then I'm suddenly remembering how I helped
deliver the four pigs to the Blayney abattoir that time.
Dawn shadows flickering over the ute, as it rattled
the frosty, hawthorn-hemmed road, driving in
from a friend's hobby-farm. ('Not much of a "hobby"
for the poor pigs,' as the old joke goes.) The animals
packed tight, morosely rocking in the cage on the back.
Then, a quarter of a kilometre or so out from the slaughter
house, their suddenly setting up an uncanny shriek,
as if intuiting what was coming for them. Shrilling eerily
aloud: with a sense of deep-seated grievance at being so
ill-used, almost. Thus skewering us on the metaphor
which we stole for our language from them, and 'Squealing
like the stuck pigs' they would shortly become.

Shaming me to be part of that day's filthy work—
as, with the deed done, we bore the empty cage
rattling hollowly home. And I flexed my chilled
fingers in their woollen gloves, pretending my hands
were clean. With that terrible sound still scalding
my eardrums—so that I could almost never eat pork,
ham or bacon again.

Tiliqua scinoides as viewed from space

Like us, when cornered, Tiliqua might seek to intimidate by aggrandising itself: puffing itself up, opening its mouth and hissing. But its bite is not venomous—its teeth are engineered for crushing not tearing, and rarely break the skin.

This creature inclines to a modest home range of garden paths, rockeries, shrubs and ponds. If inhabiting your front yard, your back yard will be alien terrain: a country for which it has no passport.

Like any old car of a cold Canberra morning, Tiliqua needs warming up in the sun to start. In high summer, the creature is sun-smart: avoiding the extreme part of the day, making recourse to plant cover and PVC pipes for shade.

As with the case of its creature-colleagues the Snow Leopard and Blue Whale, legislation protects this animal. It is illegal to cage it, to sell it as a pet, or to in any way interfere with it in the wild.

It is shamefully anthropocentric ('degenerate', you could say) to saddle any wild creature with a 'pet' human name. But if you must, then choose Classical Greco-Roman ones for Tiliqua males (Hector, Victor, Caligula, Ajax...); and, for females, names hailing from the antebellum American Confederate states (Scarlett, Suellen—Annabelle, Aunt Pittypat). Alternatively, the Habsburgs might serve at a pinch (Maximilian, Franz-Joseph, Rudolf—Eleonora, Wilhelmina, Theresa-Magdalena or such). But for reasons of cultural sensitivity too complex to go into here now, please steer clear of: Guido, Cornelius, Jedda ... Marilyn, Tallulah, Prudence, Igor or Brian. Raeleen, Nadine and Stacey. And likewise Siobhan (actually pronounced 'Shee-Vorn'). And keep your hands right off of 'Tyrone', I've got dibs on that myself.

Being an intrinsically unathletic animal, Tiliqua predates on whatever less nimble creatures than itself it might find. Slower-moving varieties of beetles, caterpillars, bugs, slugs and snails. And the more docile varieties of fruit-&-vegetables: strawberries, tomatoes, dates, and chokos, avoiding faster-paced, more aggressive models like red radishes, spring onions and kale.

During mating season (September to November), eligible Tiliqua males will court multiple females within a 15-houseblock range. Injuries (cuts, bites, scars and bruising) from over-robust love-play can and will occur. Gestation is 3 to 5 months; with sexual maturity attained around 3 years of age.

Sadly, this animal lacks sufficient streetsmartz to avoid ingestion of snail-baits—so best desist filling your garden with those. Just be honest, and ask yourself: 'Why expect a Blue Tongue to enjoy poisoning itself, any more than you would, or anyone else?'

Once determined that you're no actual threat to it (if in fact you actually aren't), Tiliqua should nicely settle down, to tantalisingly reveal itself. Opening up for you like a hibiscus flower at summer dawn, or a cultivated glasshouse rose.

If so privileged as to have Tiliqua stray into your home, be aware that it doesn't appreciate roughhouse: being lifted and rudely manhandled, losing its contact with the ground. Younger specimens will protest such impertinence by impetuously jettisoning their tail, to subsequently regrow from the stump. In order to safely return Tiliqua outdoors, carefully nudge it into a shoe box, or tenderly gather it up in a towel.

For this animal's further general wellbeing, always double-check your vehicle's rear-view mirror when reversing out the drive. Be aware (and I will only say this the once): It is malignant, and in fact technically illegal, to deliberately run over a Blue Tongue which is basking in the road. (Constituting a 'coward-punch' of sorts: you should bloody well feel ashamed!) Along similar lines, gardening implements (mowers—both hand-type, and ride-ons—whipper snippers, hedge trimmers and chainsaws) should be kept on tight leash; or better still completely garaged. And, in consideration of sensitivity to noise and fumes—for Tiliqua and everyone else in the neighbourhood: Have you ever considered using a simple rake, instead of a fucking leaf-blower?

Key Tiliqua predators include: brown falcons, currawongs, kookaburras—and the 'usual-suspect' mulga snakes, red-bellies and eastern-browns. But your own cats and dogs will nicely do the job—and are principal cause, in fact, for most suburban Blue Tongue young failing to attain adulthood. (And, as ever, Derrrrrh!: It is You, as apex predator, who constitute the greatest danger by far—to Tiliqua and every other poor living-thing else across the face of this benighted Earth.)

With due attention given to all points above—improved nutrition, and medical advances of recent decades, and the usual helpful stiff shot of good luck—Tiliqua's present numbers might thus just possibly be sustained. Five years from now, W.H.O. figures optimistically project that average life expectancy for first-world Blue Tongue males could be 30 years, say. And 35 years for females, perhaps.

Finally, on a parting note: Michael Collins, for my money the most personable and 'human' of the astronauts, with the most consistently interesting things to say—see his celebrated Apollo Mission memoir, *Carrying the Fire* (50th anniversary edition 2019; original edition 1974)—attested to feeling both humbled and profoundly moved by sight of his first Tiliqua from space. Describing the animal's projected tongue as 'nearest to Pacific Blue', on the paint-chart. And the creature appearing every bit as beautiful, fragile and precious as this great-wobbly, whorling planet of ours itself (he'd probably have added, if those press conference lardheads had bothered to ask)—as it blithely hurtles its way on, headstrong, across the vast, dark, existential void.

The prayer thief: a postscript

('Wing and a prayer')

Before the prayer-flags finally fail and I have
to tear them down, they've got this one last trick
in them to turn. Namely: entice a wattlebird
to encumber itself, dangling upside-down,
thrashing like a 3 lb fighting fish on a line,
in the rag-shop of their faded cloth. So at first I thought
the thing ensnared, and was just making moves
to untangle it, when—by sudden and dramatic
sleight-of-hand (starkly erupting from within
them like a violent sneeze)—the bird detached,
and freed itself. And with a chary, sidewards look,
shot off in a vigorous wing-burst! Skedaddling itself
long-and-low, bouncing over our back fence
like a skipped stone. With a snatch of cloth, borne
meek as a fat-flopping moth, held scissored in its beak.

Material for feathering its nest, as I presume.
With this further curious fact on top: Namely, that
in its half-dozen return sallies to the crime scene,
of the five flag colours palely proffering
themselves there, the bird-perp (for reasons best
known to itself) chooses to purloin the *white*-coloured
prayer-cloth. Privileging it above the blue, yellow,
green or red as evidently more copacetic in hue.
Better-purposed, or more providentially blessed?
More thoroughly impregnated with prayer-text?
Or best fitted, via its near translucency, to expressing
the sheer, giddying allure of Sky or the Godhead?

In any case: whichever the above, being far away
the best-coloured material for a parent wattlebird to filch,
to insulate its wattle-chick's nest.

Ducks, Lake Vembanad

(Kerala)

Rounding the lake bend
we come on a sudden pestilence of ducks:
stretched in a great looping swathe,
right across our *kettuvallam*'s path.
500 strong at least: besieging us like the massed
tractor-trucks of protesting farmers
blockading a Delhi avenue.
With three men, each stood in his runtish
wooden canoe, balancing himself with a barging pole
suspended horizontally in arm.
With the look of a surreal cowboy,
herding and corralling his flock-stock.

The nearest one, in sagging white *dhoti*,
extends his long poling stick
to single an arbitrary, handier bird out
from the mottled brown multitude.
Threshes, flails, then briskly clocks
it over the head. Poles himself closer—
crouches and reaches out
to retrieve its sorry, limp, broken body,
then drop it into his craft
like a small child's lost gumboot.

His dinner, I presume?
Wouldn't mind a taste of Lake Vembanad duck
myself, if he might care to share it with me.
Here, at this azure-lapping lake's great spread.
This fare so bountifully harvested
from Kerala's big blue-bayou.

FOURTEEN

9 Sonnets

The willow-slayers

(Yarramundi Reach, Lake Burley Griffin)

They are conducting a vendetta here, against
my favourite tree: this bankside strewn with piles of
sawn limbs, like the outside of a Civil War hospital tent.
They have gone at it something fierce, with a vengeance
terrible to see: exterminating it root and branch—
making a charnel house all along this creek.
Chain-sawed the things down to knee-high stumps,
then bulldozed those up out of the ground too.
Upending them wholesale—to thoroughly cleanse themselves
of this tree, and ensure it will never come back.
Why do they hate it so much? What do these people so fear?
For, as I gaze on this scene of unrelieved slaughter,
it's an incontrovertible truth:
They are terrible willow-haters here!

Chalk stream

(Overton, UK)

Chalk streams rise from chalk bedrock, to flow
through chalk hills to the sea. They have preternatural
clarity. Are startling and pristine: like Earthrise viewed
from the moon. Their spring-fed waters are shallow
and wide—mineral-rich, alkaline and clean. (Commonly
described as 'gin clear'.) They have stable flow, constant
temperature, and are generally weed-free: ideal
for production of watercress; and, in their upper reaches,
for dry-fly fishing. 160 of the world's 210 chalk streams
are located in England, including this one on whose bank we stand
now: the River Test at Overton, on the Jane Austen Tourist
Trail from Chawton to Winchester, in Hampshire.
And we're much impressed—though, to be frank, never having
actually heard of a 'chalk stream' at all, prior to visiting here.

The hail cars

The cars of Canberra are warehoused
in a rented field. Gridlocked: pressed bumper-to-bumper,
and door-to-door. Sardined in the grassy khaki,
as if gathered on the Red Sea's shore
and awaiting benevolent crossing
to the Land of Spare Parts; or re-birth
in some second-hand car saleyard.
Their enamel skins pocked, as if sounded all over
with geological hammers. Shattered windscreens
and side-windows. Damaged in their tender parts—
with Hope a crash-test dummy, strapped riding
stiffly within them. As they're stranded in their parked
Purgatory here: instead of being free to kick their heels up,
out there—cruising the open road.

Apricot drop: the derelict orchard, Armidale

For Skye

The fruit drops to rot at the field's edge,
alongside the old post-and-rail fence
which the cattle have broken through
to stand hock-high in the bleached khaki grass.
Heads lowered, to snuffle the gooey muck up
in long, slender blue lasso tongues:
gorging themselves on dropped apricots.

And you step among, bearing a bucket
to salvage some small amount of this blighted crop
(windfall of a derelict orchard): for stewing, or making
jam. Though leaving the greater part to be tromped
under-hoof on the ground, and hoovered up as cattle slop.
Yes, well: In the evident absence of bread or cake—
Let the cattle eat apricots!

Snow gums (the ridge)

That tangle of snow gums set high on the ridge
forms a lovely, languorous backdrop, as the fire
hobbles steadfastly across the heath towards them.
Like a huddle of wind-bent blondes: formed up
in arabesques, their sheeny-cream shoulders bared
and dropped, as they stare coolly back at the flames.
Lingering at the edge of this great, dangerous game—
as if inviolable, safe above it all. Oblivious of the fact
of their potent, oiled wood-grain, and the real peril
the fire presents for them. Fool-fuel that they are. That,
in an instant their entire neighbourhood might ignite—
and detonate. Like Soweto, Redfern, or Watts. Delhi in 1984.
Brixton, 1995. Paris, 1968. Just be sent spectacularly tottering
up, in thick-reaming, red-blue-&-black caterwauls of flame.

Economic rationalism hits the zoo

The year that Covid closed the Zoo,
sorely depleting it of funds,
the management was forced to some hard decisions
on how to feed its animals. And, subverting
the cliched paradigm
of the Natural World's food chain
(which elects to pander to the 'elite beasts'
so-called, and work from the 'top-feeders' down)
took a refreshing, revolutionary approach.
Which is how it came that, under strict protocols
overseen by the principal vet,
the ears were sliced off the polar bear,
then diced and fried up in a peanut-butter sauce
to feed the Brazilian marmosets.

The Cardinal

The cardinal—dressed sharp in gunslinger black,
homburg hat, and aviator sunglasses—sips an espresso
at the pavement table of his favourite Roman café.
Surrendering himself to the sun, as it lulls him back
to cicadary summers in the magic-faraway of his days
as a young diocesan priest. And the laughs of a garland
of boys echoing off the changeroom tiles of a regional
city swimming pool: Halleluiahing upward
in a swallow-swirl which does his poor, ailing heart well.
Makes him feel vital and whole; powerful, and purposeful
again. As he now stiffly rises to pay—
then bearishly ambles his way off to his task
penetrating the Curia's deep, dark-tangled finances.
Doing God's good work today.

The 'Fisher-of-Men' is a 'Fisher-of-Women' too

(Sunday morning, Empire Bay, NSW)

Stroked their way through mist-tangled waters to the point,
the women haul their kayak up onto the bank, then climb
the grassy hill to the small, sandstone church. Lean oars
by the door, tug their paddling boots off, and step in ...
Their bare feet and boating clothes draw the odd side look,
but the pair are accepted readily enough for their help
filling out the empty pews. As outside, meanwhile, the tide's
on the move: munching on the mangrove's green-brown
spikey stalks in a gentle-tippling ruck-&-maul ... Here,
on this gleaming broadwater teeming with snapper, flathead
and bream. Back across which the women will duly stroke
home. And into which they sometimes incline to drop a line
themselves. In this place where, by basic principle of equal right,
the 'Fisher of Men' must be a 'Fisher of Women' as well.

Rumination: the cattle

(Corryong, Victorian Alps)

Stood patient, pressed shoulder-to-shoulder,
crimped deep in eucalypt shadow,
the cattle have gathered to ruminate
on the great question
which has hung over their fields
and heads for millennia
like the Damoclean sword.

Namely: Is it better for them
to have been bred
to wait daily
for slaughter like this?
Or for them to have never been born
to live out their sordid lives as cattle
at all?

TWO BUCOLICS

The Darling at Menindee

(Bucolic with two offered endings)

This is how a river looks, when down to its true
business in Australia's great inland. No idyll frippery
(*'pleasaunce'*): cheap light-tricks on grassy banks,
effete effects of willowy romance—Just the hard,
reported truth, and bare facts of the whole vital,
unstoppable thing. With the river bulldozed
through the scene like slum clearance, to create
a chaos of savage, scarred, ravaged upheaval.
A cross between a riverscape and a war zone:
ochry khaki-browns, sore yellows and cementish-greys.
High-tottering, dried-out mudbanks like bomb-busted
berms. River redgums smashed onto their sides,
poking awrily up at the sky, like spiked field guns
from some long-gone Somme battlefield. Messes
of smaller branches, twigs, and scalped leaf-clumps
choking the trees' lower forks—to evidence some prior
flood event of a scale and degree of rage which it's
impossible to conceive could ever come roiling its way
in through here now; in these still times. The empty,
torn-up riverbed looking to have been dynamited—
like some Central African construction works
to lay a highway. Which a river, of course, essentially is
(or at least, traditionally *was*). Though you'd be hard put
to jemmy even a canoe in through this landscape
in these present droughty times. Pretty well be *portage*:
limping, dragging and scraping the thing from green
skanky pool to skanky green pool the whole way …

Ending 1:

Yet for all of this, the river gums persevere—
sending down their modest, tangled roots
to grapple hold, and make the best stand that
they can. And a few token and astonishingly
fragile things dress the dun-coloured heaviness
with almost inadvertent delicacy and grace;
as if laughing in the bleak face of it. This
scissor-grinder pair for instance, frolicking
the branch of that toppled gum. Skittering,
chippering and busying themselves in the dusk
light; doing their gentle thing. Then, as we set
our camp chairs up around the fire, a pelican pair
appears. Beating their way tirelessly abreast—making
slow, diligent progress from some evident expedition
down below the riverbend. Startlingly clean-and-bright
as tennis whites, against this vast, crushing and
amorphous dun-coloured terrain. Winging companionably
along in gentle tandem. Steadfast—all 'hail-fellow-well-met'.
Like a pair of sage-eyed idols, with unflappable
command etched into the broad downstroke of each
unharried wingbeat—as they pace themselves
in their desert-country marathon. Putting fresh breath
into this entire, devastated and exhausted scene,
as they glide on past us now at roof-level height.
Breasts gilded by the 'Golden Hour'.
Out here, at Menindee.

Ending 2:

Then, as we linger on the bank, a pelican pair skulk
in around the big arid, empty car-lot of the riverbend.
Beating their dogged way: catafalque-party grim and slow.
Hulking, humpbacked—gaunt, despondent.
Ashamed-looking, almost. Prognathous with great,
heavy beaks—and, with their arduous, predatory lope,
abjectly Jurassic in both look and feel. Seeming to drag
an ominous foreboding in their train. Out here, deep in
these stalled claypan doldrums of the western plains
outback. Where we stand beside this scrap of broken
river desperately holding out in anaerobic
cul-de-sacs; forming a chain-gang of limpid,
chartreuse-coloured puddles ... Then turn our backs
to leave the derelict campsite, and drive on somewhere
further for the night. Right out of sight of this cowed
river's thin slop of filthy water: with its pallid, reeking
bouillabaisse of glaze-eyed, haemorrhaging fish-flesh,
piled up so thick that it gives like an obscene trampoline
if walked upon. To rupture underfoot.
Out here, at Menindee.

If Nappa Merrie was the Berkshire Downs: a conjectural

Nappa Merrie: cattle station, 7,275 square kilometres, located in Channel Country straddling SW Queensland/South Australian border, and incorporating Cooper Creek protected 'Dig Tree' historical site

1.

If Nappa Merrie was the Berkshire Downs: there'd be no need
for lignum, gidgee trees or Mitchell grass to indicate the line
of that dry watercourse. These 'jump-ups' would be grassy
meadow land—smothered in Bluebells, Buttercups, Vetches,
Clovers, Cowslips and Orchids. And—for these Little Crows,
Zebra Finches, Budgerigars, Mulga Parrots and Galahs
seen winging all about the place, we might substitute, say:
Skylarks, Cuckoos, Partridges—Thrushes, Swifts or Nightingales.

Bore 23 might be some medieval saint's sacred
healing-well, offering present-day refreshment
to weary ramblers on an old pilgrimage trail—to Glastonbury,
or wherever. And it wouldn't take our kind host Dave
an entire day almost, to negotiate a 500-kay-long, dusty
circuit in his LandCruiser to show us just a sample third
of his property's entire area; checking his occasional
fencelines, and stock of Brahmin-cross Hereford and
Angus, clinging to their watering tanks. (And moreover,
given the natural proliferation of downland rivers,
brooks, streams and rills—there'd be no parched
cattle even out here actually *craving* water, anyway.)

Feral camels wouldn't ghost the far, flat, dusty, mirage-humped
horizon like some cutting-room floor outtake from *Lawrence*

of Arabia. Nor bandit gangs of donkeys traipse untidily about
the place like stage props purloined from San Jose or Tijuana.
Instead, what we'd be looking at is: Voles, Moles, Hedgehogs,
Squirrels (both red and grey in kind), Badgers, and a host of
other suchlike fauna more properly indigenous and appropriate to
an English southern-downs landscape.

2.

If Nappa Merrie was the Berkshire Downs: we wouldn't happen
on a dingo pack, circling a baby camel fraily struggling to
its wonky legs—with its mother shouldering in, her big,
thick-muscled neck careening close and low, protectively
in over it—as she looked off darkly sidewards, nostrils
flared, to sniff the murdering air. And I would not have felt
that prurient urge to pull my camera phone, and snap the image
of those five calves, mummified and so photogenically posed,
laid out in the stony river bed. (There from the previous year's
drought—or was it actually, Dave said, the flash flood two years
prior to that?) Sight of which, tantalisingly exotic and dramatic
as it was for me, was hardly something Dave or his wife Kim—
as property owners who had grown the beasts—wanted
to be reminded of; less still needed to see.

3.

If Nappa Merrie was the Berkshire Downs: then Burke & Wills
would be another tale entirely, of course. With the pair not
direly struggled their way through such vast, bleak, dry,
hostile and loveless terrain. But rather just perambulated
verdant fields, never far from some free-running water source—
with fat lambs freely beckoning from pastures and companionably

to hand for ready slaughter. And a cornucopia of wild fruits—
strawberries, raspberries, blueberries, barberries—rosehips,
cherries, sloes and damsons—not to mention chanterelle
and other mushroom titbits flaunting themselves,
available for the taking: for foraging from forest, field, coppice
and hedgerow, should hunger even remotely call.

With all of this just making it a *cinch* for the Expedition
party to haul its way straight up through to the Gulf—then turn
about to dawdle amiably back south to home, for fete and glory.
If considerably *less* glory though, you'd reckon: bereft of their
romantic aura and *cachet* of heroic if disaster-prone explorers,
as mythologised today. Denied the flavour of intrigue—
the contextual 'colour', and piquant sense of 'barely-missed'
survival. And the compelling, tragic atmospherics
which have underlaid and generated so much vital art,
music and literature in the broken wake of their benighted,
real-world, expeditionary feat.

And so, *ipso facto* too, of course: this celebrated 'Dig Tree'
which Dave's LandCruiser has delivered us to now—rather
than being the tottering, propped, half-rotted coolabah
cum mega tourist-magnet which it is—might be some
more run-of-the-mill English-downlands tree type:
like a Willow, Birch, or Alder; Ash or Oak. And—just
to extrapolate this whole concept further: lonely, stony
Tibooburra, marooned in its granite-gibbet outcrops
six hours drive (426 kilometres) south-east down through
the Dog Fence—wouldn't sport the artful memorial
sculpture modelled on Sturt's upturned whaleboat,
to emblemise some similar 'Heroic-Romantic' (or 'Naïve-Ironic'?)
failure. Because, given typical, endemic English-downland-type

rainfall, and the consequent high water-table, an annual
Henley-style regatta (commemorating Sturt perhaps,
as inaugural Commodore?) might feature on the grassy shores
of his ersatz great 'Inland Sea' today.

4.
Yes, well, anyway. It's a thought—if completely fanciful, okay.
To imagine all of this could be some different, tamer, vastly
gentler, more amenable landscape. With permanent lush pasture;
ponds, and wending brooks at beck-and-call. Copses and hedgerows.
Fields criss-crossed with chalk-pathed fields, filled with grains
and stock. Which, to take just half a look around, it adamantly *isn't*,
and patently never could remotely ever be … As sunset now
raddles coffee-coloured Cooper Creek, a stone's throw beyond
the homestead's garden fence. And we sip Sav-Blanc and Cab-Merlot
on the small, reticulation-fed back lawn, and await the barbecue.
Absorbing the dusk-shadowed grandeur of this vast Channel Country,
slowly welling darkly up all round—to be impaled by desert stars.
And this land insistently continues to be every bit just simply
what it is. And it must be.

So best we just get over it I guess and suck it up.

HISTORY & FABLES

An inquisitor reports his good work to his cardinal back home

(Homage à Ken Russell)

Eminence—
        Regrettably I am obliged to report
that the nuns are at it again. *En masse*, and with a real
vengeance. Rolling over-and-over on their backs
across the chapel floors, in a tangle of black-and-white.
Completely ga-ga: goggle-eyed as horses,
and jibbering in tongues. Carolling, chanting,
and flapping their paws like seals, in their 'ecstatic'
seizures (or 'visions', so-called). Rending the cloth
of their scapulars and exposing their breasts.
Ruching their habits up, to claw at their thighs.
Indulging in the most wanton, unlicensed fondling
and self-pleasuring of themselves.

We have witnessed some truly astonishing sights.
Last week we encountered a novice with nipples
on her the size of unpitted Cycladean olives. (And of similar
texture and hue.) And the amount of hair sometimes seen
to be growing down there can be scandalous—uncanny,
and hard to credit. (Though allegedly quite normal for a
mature woman, my deacon assures. Outside my area
of expertise there, I confess.) Yesterday, while conducting
a search of some novitiates' dormitories, we uncovered
a stash of lewd drawings inscribed upon vellum from beneath
their beds. And a box of devices (including one of
improbable size in both length and girth) confected
from wood, bone and vegetable. With which these

creatures evidently console themselves when in their *extremis*,
the Mother Superior advised.

Yes—just as the Good Book teaches, Eminence, there's
no limit to the depth of God's Mystery. It's a damned
rich and exhausting business we conduct, I can tell you.
Dire, occasionally *perilous*. But we persevere nonetheless—
prosecuting our righteous cause; keeping rigid
faith in this urgent and necessary work. And I'm happy
to say that, with due application of appropriate prayers, rites
and supplications, we have managed to save some pleasing
fair number of offenders outright. Harder-boiled cases
naturally require stripping, binding and recourse to the brand
or scourge. And, as ever, the hard-bitten recidivist few
remain simply rotten to their devilish core. For whom,
alas, we've no practicable option but to mercifully consign to
the flames or put to the sword.

It's a pretty unsavoury business, all in all. Galling, onerous.
Certainly taking its toll—and quite frankly not always
garnering the gratitude from the women that you'd expect
it ought. Sometimes these wretches seem the living
end, and I fear they might do me in. For we still have far
to go in this Dark Night—so many more establishments
to visit and venture our way through, in pursuit of this
sacred work. But fret not, Eminence! We've broad shoulders,
steady hands and stout hearts, God's stalwarts as we are.
And must just do our best in any case—at the most propitious
possible pace, and with God's grace—day-by-day.
Maintaining our strength for as long as we can, in assurance
that Goodness shall prevail. And that, by Heaven's rigor,
these women be made to submit: To kneel, and kiss
the stern rod of God.

'Needs Must When the Devil Drives,' as the proverb goes.
To which end: Keep us close in your thoughts, won't you
Eminence. And fast in your prayers too, needless to say.
As we pursue this great and essential, if exhausting
and seemingly endless work with all possible zeal.
And I remain, as ever,

> *In our Redeemer's name,*
> *and for Righteousness' sake,*
> *ever-obediently yours,*

——— ———

[*Correspondence signed and stamped
with the Provost's seal*]

The 'Battle for Berlin' (The Zoo)

If things in Berlin weren't going too well for the High
Command, battened down in their Fuhrerbunker
over those final 12 months of the War, it was hardly a picnic
for the animals in the City Zoo either—just across the
Tiergarten down the way. Prolonged Allied bombing had
already forced leopards, jaguars, panthers and lions to abandon
their pulverised cages. Seen trapped monkeys screaming
in burning treetops, and snakes slithering in a blind
panic into parks, private gardens and any quieter, safer
surrounding green space they might find. All manner and
variety of crazed and dazed animals were exposed to plain
view, wandering Zombie-like in the city's blitzed streets.
And necessitating deployment of scarce Wehrmacht resources
sorely needed elsewhere for their hunting down. To be either
captured or shot.

In the wash up, just 91 of the Zoo's 3,715 pre-conflict animals
survived the 'Battle for Berlin'. Among them: two lions,
two hyenas, ten hamadryas baboons, an Asian bull elephant
named 'Siam', the celebrity hippo bull 'Knautschke',
the chimpanzee 'Empress Suse'—and a single (and, so far as
can be ascertained) unnamed black stork. The extent to which
the Nazi elite huddled underground several blocks away
appreciated or were even actually aware of their animal-neighbours'
plight is not known. But to be fair to the Nazis, their hands
were pretty full by these dark days: struggling with the multiple,
complex issues of the conflict, and the more specific personal
consequences each for themselves … Joseph and Magda
Goebbels, for instance, caring for their six children in the family

bunker-bedroom. Sedating them before crushing cyanide capsules in their mouths. Then having to make their own fraught, final emotional farewell to the Fuhrer and traipse off to top themselves. And let's not forget that the Fuhrer had to put down his beloved Alsatian, 'Blondi' (making recourse to some handy cyanide too). Not to mention Eva's own delicate and testing personal situation as virtual instantaneous ('impromptu') bride-cum-widow, to be factored into it as well. Christ, things were pretty tough all round! It's not as if the Nazis couldn't empathise with the overwhelming sense of loss and tragic waste which was blindly staggering the world. (You'd *presume*.) Didn't shoulder their *own* fair share and burden, or were somehow magically 'immune' to the suffering and sacrifice too ... Let's just say that such matters were a general permeating presence and prevailing concern in the gritty-grey, cordite-and-smoke choked air—and '*Zeitgeist*', as it were—of Berlin around that time.

The 'Battle for Crete'

'Ajax' is a brand of Greek classical hero,
a well-known, patented household cleanser …
And a Leander-class Royal Navy light-cruiser
renowned for its front-page exploits in helping sink
the German raider the *Graf Spee* at the River Plate,
in December 1939. And aboard which my 20-year-old father
served as a CPO during the 'Battle for Crete' and subsequent
five-day 'Withdrawal' in May 1941.
Which saw the Royal Navy, in face of overwhelming
enemy airpower, suffer loss of a great number
of ships and men.

Ajax was obliged to withdraw from the 'Withdrawal'
when her main shaft and rudder were damaged
in a 'Near Miss' from a Stuka bomb, off Heraklion—
and limp back to Alexandria for repairs. And 40 years
later, in a coach tour of Victoria's Great Ocean Road,
my father got talking with an English veteran
whose platoon had been captured on a Crete beach
when a Royal Navy cruiser tasked with taking them off
had never showed. So Dad was able to explain why.

> 'I spent the whole rest of the war as a POW
> in Germany before getting back to my wife in England,
> on account of you!' was the veteran's riposte.

But his wife (with a 'pretty dry sense
of humour', as Dad described) reached out
to shake Dad's hand, and smiled: 'Thank you mister,
for giving me those four years of peace!'

Ajax and Dad parted ways after Crete:
Dad being posted to an Egyptian shore base,
and *Ajax* undertaking an extensive refit
before returning as part of 'Force K' on D-Day
and firing the first salvos on German gun emplacements
on Gold Beach. Post-war, she served in the Palestine
Patrol and was involved in the '*Exodus* Incident'—
before her eventual decommissioning in February 1948.
She was slated for sale to the Chilean Navy,
but Churchill intervened—and rather than see
the great lady diminished by some servile role
off foreign shores, ordered that she be sent to scrap.
(A more honourable ending in naval terms, evidently.
Akin to being borne from the battlefield on your shield,
like Ajax's legendary comrade Achilles, at Troy.)
So she was broken up in the yards at South Wales,
in November 1949.
Dad went on for some 63 years more. And when he passed
in June 2012, we slipped his ashes into the sea off a northern
Sydney beach. As he'd requested—and as likewise seemed,
for the small huddle of participants gathered there in the rain—
as with the instance of his old ship—the most fit and proper
course of action, and 'honourable' conclusion to proceedings, too.

Thylacine stomp

(film footage of last known Thylacine, filmed Beaumaris Zoo, Hobart, 1933)

Tiger stripes set G-string low on lap-dancer
hips, and cinched in tight around the swollen base
of your kangaroo-like tail, you make these switchback
moves. Tripping the scratchy-grey monotone of your
cage's confines in a dark fandango set to some wobbly
metronome's offbeat. Then suddenly haul to, turn
your gaping, lacrosse-racquet jaw straight to camera
and—talk about 'cool under fire'—appear to actually
yawn! (If more likely uttering some muted kind
of whine or bush-yowl?) Then, just as the footage judders
and flickers right out, take that one sudden, further,
giddy, momentous, razor-thin sidewards step—
to evanesce. And vamoose yourself, lickety-split!

Shockingly disappeared: like that stunt with the Banksy
print chewed up in the auctioneer's shredding machine.
Expunged from the habitat you intrinsically owned,
and purposefully roamed—to which you so *natively*
belonged, and had every due cause to be in.
Shrivelled up in one great, convulsing spasm of flame
and black smoke, as if that nitrate film documenting
you had been put to the match. Instantly hurtled back,
into the long-lost Pleistocene from which you had come.
Leaving us all stood flatfooted here, bereft—gawping
dumbfucks, in the acrid stench of our sanctuary outside
your cage. Exiled alone: with just the teasing remnant,
and flickering ghost of our shaky few dozen metres of shonky
film footage preserved—to bear testimony to your once
having miraculously been.

Orison for Oates

(Captain Lawrence 'Titus' Oates: 1880-1912)

Ponting's glass photoplate shows you posed midships
by the stalls of four white Manchurian ponies,
with two sleeping huskies balled up at your feet—
as the *Terra Nova*, streaming its black-steam pennant
plume, bucks, shudders and heaves its way south
into a rising squall.

Ashore, you dutifully performed your tasks,
and tended the ponies: their four legs scrabbling
on the ice, you limping accompanying upon
your two own. (Which were of uneven length—
with the left leg healed an inch shorter than the right,
from a shattered thigh in the South African Wars.)
Despite your reservations of Scott, and more so
the vainglory of his grand Polar March—
you agreed to take part when selected. Leading
the ponies to lay the depots—then watching
them successively fail: 'Nobby', 'Chinaman', 'Jehu',
'Bones'. And then, when your own pony 'Christopher'
failed too, defying tradition you insisted on putting
him down yourself ... Before the party struggled
up over the Beardmore Glacier, and then all the way on:
to discover themselves Amundsen's also-rans
on arrival at the Pole itself.

The return march revived your old war wounds.
Your feet turned gangrenous, you lost use of both hands,
and increasingly fell behind—till eventually,
in the bravura gesture to be bellowed for decades
from every *Boys' Own*, you stepped out from the tent

into a bawling storm as white as the pale-whipped manes
of those stumbling ponies which Scott brought
all this giddy way south. To perish so far from their
native home.
And, in like spirit of sacrifice to theirs,
put yourself down on the cold ice too.

Postscript: the shifting graves

The search party that found the three in the tent
at 'One Ton' neglected to find trace of you.
So erected a cairn judged nearest the spot to where your
loss was presumed. But over subsequent years
in any case—in consort with the bodies of Scott,
Wilson and Bowers—your remains (with the two
legs of uneven length: the right an inch longer
than the healed left, from injury in the South African
Wars—and perhaps along with the scrambling bones
of the butchered Manchurian ponies as well?)
would likely have long been carried off
in the travelling ice's inexorable ruck-and-maul.
To be delivered to, and collectively sunk,
in the same bleak, lonely, gaping graveyard
of the cold Ross Sea.

Beechey Island

(Franklin Expedition, 1845)

1.
Full points for perseverance—hauling themselves all the way
out here, to this stony beach in the Arctic waste.
Three thousand kilometres from respectable population,
and some 140 years post the event. (Though a twin-engine
Otter makes it a cinch, against the coal-fired, wooden ships
that we lumbered our way in upon.) Then again for their digging
through a metre-and-a-half of shaly permafrost: 36 hours,
three men swinging the pick in turns, to reveal my box.
Then wrangle it out, jemmy open the lid to disclose my
mummified corpse. Boil up buckets of snow to pour
onto the ice caul shrouding my head and shoulders. Peel
back the red kerchief to expose my raw, livid face: lips braced
back over wide-gapped teeth in a kind of giddy leer.
Looking like a drunk man in a wind-tunnel test. Big bared
eyeballs staring hard out and popped with unseeing—
blinded by incessant close reading of unrelenting permafrost.
(A century-and-a-half of Arctic conditions will induce
that kind of expression, yes?) Then lifting me rigid
from the crate, to lie me on the stony ground. Noting
the care which my crewmates had shown in my original
burying: cushioned on a bed of the ship's-carpenter's
woodchips; togged out in three layers of clothing,
woollen cap tugged down snug on my head. (If admittedly
having fudged ceremony a bit by wrestling my left arm
in under my back and forcing the angle of my legs,
to make me fit the box.)

They certainly brought some expertise and expensive
equipment to dig a simple seaman up.
Radiology—Pathology—A period clothing specialist.
Plus camera and sound gear for recording it all. X-raying me.
Taking biopsy samples for consumption and pneumonia—snippets
of my hair, bone and nails to test for lead. Before stripping
me bare, and stretching my clothing out flat on the ground
alongside me like the extended wings of a broken albatross.
Cataloguing everything meticulously down to the individual
buttons, the sewing of the seams and hems, and weave of the
cloth. Then finally, with all this done, popping me crisply
back in my box to reconsign me to the frozen ground.
Consulting their pre-excavation drawings, to get the
re-interment exact: putting me safely back, locked under the
same proper, big, flat, carefully-coded stones.
('Nothing to see here folks! Move along!')
Before the sound of shovelled gravel, clattering like hail on top.
Which just left the dull murmur of the returning
Twin-Otter heard straining in low over the sea again,
to reload them and all their expensive equipment up
and bear it and them away … Off back to the vital,
throbbing South and its superabundance of glutting sun.
Which, extraneous to say, I'd have given an arm
and a leg to have been able to safely return to myself.
Back in the day.

2.
But why this great and extravagant undertaking in the
first place? Tracking our spoor all this arduous way
north? This terrible compulsion to dig matters up,
instead of just leave sad matters to lie? ... A pox on the
perpetual prurience of humankind—whether under
the head of 'History', 'Science' or whatever proposed cause
or name. The least return a man should expect for his
trouble in venturing all the way out here, to perish
and be left lying for a century-and-a-half in this
godforsaken place, would be some decent quiet; and
the right for his body to lie undisturbed. (You'd think.)
Pray Christ!: Now that the ghouls have dug me up twice
and have just located the wreck of the *Erebus*, they'll
fixate on that from now on. And we three can be left to
get on with our solitary lingering in peace. Here, together
alone—succoured on metre-deep permafrost,
under the Arctic skies. And they won't need to ever return
to do such filthy work again.

Frankly, with hindsight—if I got caught up in
similar adventuring again, with a choice between burying
or burning at the end—I'd opt for cremation next time.
To prevent the thugs rupturing my hard-won composure—
and deny the mad, interfering buggers the pleasure
(or hobby) of meddling with my flesh and bones.

Eagle debriefing: still life

When Armstrong backflipped
off the edge of the Earth,
his boot-prints were mass-produced
in plaster-cast and diminishing sizes,
to dance with the plaster ducks
down our livingroom walls.

A wired-up Stars-and-Stripes
was left behind, like the outstretched wing
of a badly taxidermied bird;
or the sound of one hand clapping
in the moon's dead audience.

And afterwards (as was largely feared),
the sports-vehicle recreationists came
to hoon all over the grey dune-scape—
then abandon their buggies untidily up there
just parked any damned whichway
to the Earth's kerb.

Mills & Boon burned their entire back-stock
of romances in the public square;
and NASA was torched by lycanthropes.

As all the rest of us, meanwhile,
heaved and tossed in our sweaty beds.
Feeling the moon's waning magic tingle
like an amputee's phantom pain.

The pilot station: a lament

(Writers Residency, Camden Haven, April 2017)

1. The house

The pilot house is a bleary eye of cream-painted
weatherboard, blinking out into continuous rain.
Holding itself firmly to the ground on its grassy reserve,
above the spot where the old rivermouth came out—
before being strong-armed by basalt breakwalls
to tame the bar, and provide a safe kiddies'
swimming beach and small asphalt carpark.
Inside, it's all homely 1950s décor: stainless steel,
linoleum and laminex. Walls hung with the kind of
atmospheric bric-a-brac paying guests would expect.
Charts identifying signal flags; instructing on the tying
of seamen's knots, and semaphore. And on how to
describe and categorise the sea's states in variously
agitated degrees of wind and storm. Along with a
30-year-old framed newscutting commemorating
retiring of the last man to serve here. For no bed is
retained for a pilot-man at the pilot-station these days.

2. The boathouse

There's no bed for a pilot-man in the pilot-station
these days. Instead, the boathouse is made over
as venue for Arts & Crafts workshops. With a
sawn-off, man-sized length of whitewashed signal staff

preserved as memento (inspiration piece),
alongside a bleached section of whale backbone.
Fold-up chairs, a tea urn and mugs, bikkie jar
and bar fridge. Yes, it's all about writers,
painters, handcrafts—and paying guests—at the
pilot-station today. Words, and watercolours;
with the weaver's woof-and-weft eclipsed the tying
of seamen's knots … No wary eyeing of the bar,
or weather-watch maintained. No space for a pilot-man
to fit at all, at the pilot-station these days.

3. The breakwall

There's no place for a pilot-man, at the pilot-station
these days—as, following three weeks of incessant
downpour in Cyclone Debbie's tail (with Debbie
now safely spent herself, corralled in some coral
atoll off the Queensland coast further north)—
the sea is stained a strange dark-tan. And is whipped
into foam the colour of a tapped Guinness's head—
as it comes at you in the heft of a breaking wave,
to be beaten into scungy, creamy-brown curds.
Toppling like tumbleweed, head-over-heel
in the wind, to smatter the cheeks of the shore.
So you bend to scoop some up, like dirty shaving
lather held cupped in both hands. Then shake it off, to climb
the breakwall—walk to its end, and stand watching
the storm-surf crash its way onto the tangled nest
of giant, concrete tetrapods. Breathing the freshest,
headiest sea-air deep down into your lungs, relishing
all of this. As meanwhile, up on its grassy reserve

behind, gleaming in a skein of sun-splintered rain,
the pilot house holds on. Rides high and steady;
calm and strong. If with no bed whatever up there however
these days, as said, to rest the head of a pilot-man.

4. The fisherman

No bed for the head of a pilot-man, at the pilot-station
these days—as, in the late afternoon, the sun briefly
breaks through for the swallows to sport: flit, swerve,
weave and swoop in gay arabesques around the old man
banksias on the cliff edge. And the setting sun king-hits
the Kattang Reserve overlooking Wash House Beach,
smearing the headland in thick lacquers of golds and reds.
And brilliantly picks out a single, bare-chested old
fisherman in yellow towelling hat and bright titanium-white
shorts. Traipsing the sands below: stumping along with head
bowed beside the rock pools, with rod and bucket in hand.
Staggering in a sort of dazed stupor, it seems. Or entirely
lost within himself, in some transcendental revery.
Absorbed in far greater and more momentous matters
in this world than the mere hooking of fish. Instead pondering
some profound injustice or outrage, such as: How could
it be that the pilot-station has so recklessly relinquished
its good, proper work, and deprived itself of its sage
weather-eye to leave the sea unsupervised: free to
misbehave, and act at its own unruly will? And *why*,
in Christ's name, in that cream-painted bungalow
glittering up there in light rain on its grassy reserve,
is no pilot-man in residence now? With no place for
a pilot-man at all, at the pilot-station these days.

'Shoes of the Danube'

(Sculpture installation, Budapest embankment, 2005)

Shoot the shoes! Bludgeon, stab or strangle them! Kill every pair!
Men's shoes—women's, children's. Working boots, all scuffed,
torn and broken. Kiddies sandals. Dress shoes—fashionable and
buffed to a bright sheen. Why should shoes even exist!?

Pour molten iron into their throats. Then, when the mould's
cooled and set, arrange the pairs artfully on this curved
embankment of the slow-sweeping Danube. Lay flowers before
them, set winking tea-lights at their heels and toes—to sing them
along, under the high-flowing starlight. Assuring them they need
have no fear: but are cherished, and safe here. *Now.* Free to just
be their pure, true shoe-selves …

Among them, I note, these sassy stand-outs of a pair of strapped
high-heels: spitting image of a yellow-&-red leather pair that I
saw behind plate-glass back in the great shoe mountain exhibit on
the Auschwitz day-tour, last week. Now sitting in pert disarray,
bankside: as if subpoenaed to crawl all their pretty way on their
hands-and-knees from Krakow, to add their testament here.

The fall of Communism

('The Russians are coming!')

Our Slovak guide Ondrej tells that, after the Wall's fall,
he took a six-month working holiday in Seattle,
and met a rich businessman there who had purchased
a Lenin statue as conversation piece for his mansion's
grounds. When Ondrej had asked the statue's source,
it turned out to be his hometown of Poprad.
And when invited to visit, he had wept at the sight:
being reminded of his childhood games in the old town square;
and feeling homesick for Slovakia from his months away.
'I *cried!*—over a *statue of Lenin!*' he exclaims,
still mortified at the thought.

Back in the Communist heyday, he tells,
town wags had struck one night:
painting a track of red footprints
staggering their way from the statue plinth
to a pub on the square's other side;
and slinging a carry-bag of empty beer bottles
from Lenin's extended hand.

And when the statue had initially been pulled down,
it had lain on town wasteland for a year.
Being made from copper, and hollow inside,
it absorbed the day's heat and kept warm at night,
and a homeless person had crept into it
and slept there for a while.

These days, Ondrej tells, the Russians are back
in Slovakia. Cashed-up, and made welcome
at the High Tatras resorts.

> 'Russians are good when they visit in *cars*,' he smiles—
> 'but not when they visit in *tanks*!'

Afterword

Apart from the two themed collections *Vanuatu Moon* and *Canberra Light* (2011/12 and 2019 respectively) my poetry books have tended to be wide-ranging ('hotch-potch'?) in subject matter, rather than coherent, single-themed collections. They have also typically drawn on a mix of more recently written pieces and others pulled from a much larger working reserve ('cookpot') of older poems which, for various reasons, have taken longer to bring to completion.

The present collection is no exception—though, as I was gathering the poems here, I did become aware of a natural coalescing around the broad themes of Faith and Grace, and the abrogation of (or shortfall from) same: forming up around various notions of what might be deemed Hope & Devotion—Fragility & Responsibility—Privilege, Relegation, Betrayal & Loss. These themes are contextualised by our human interactions with each other, with history, with inanimate objects, and with the natural world (landscape, and animal life). And seemed to create a pleasingly natural cluster around the sentiment of this collection's title poem, 'Put Out More Prayer Flags', with its playful, vernacular-domestic expression of hope, fear and desired benevolent protection.

The positive side of the ledger is seen in evocations of straightforward human caring and empathy such as: 'Filial: the detectives', and 'The waiting: the hospice, the fisherman'; and, more symbolically (theoretically) in 'The oar'. More problematic is the voice of the begrudgingly disinterred complainant in 'Beechey Island' and, at a more troubling remove still, the bizarre, casual malignancy of the persona in 'An inquisitor reports his good work to his cardinal back home', whose privilege of position is in some way echoed centuries later in the contemporary clerical figure of 'The Cardinal'. There are two very different examples of historical reprehensibility deriving from the Second World War ('The Shoes of the Danube', and 'The Battle for Berlin'), with a Cold War era companion piece in 'The fall of Communism'. Set against these are the study of traditional historical heroics from the era of Antarctic-exploration, presented in 'Orison for Oates'; juxtaposed with the more playful '*anti*-heroic' take on space-age exploration in '*Eagle* debriefing'. Regarding inanimate objects, there is the relegation (or 'repurposing') suggested in 'The pilot-station: a lament', and the prescription for rightful, respectful and responsible playing of a musical instrument ('Instructions for playing piano').

The animal world is a particular touchstone for the collection themes. The idea of 'preferencing' is evoked in 'Privilege: the crooked duck', 'Economic rationalism hits the zoo', and 'The tiger quoll coat' (which plays on the relative 'valuing' of wild animal versus domestic dog). There is consideration of human empathy—or absence thereof—as shown toward pigs, and the humble garden blue tongue lizard ('Two songs for porcines', and '*Tiliqua scinoides* as viewed from space'); as well as the zoo animals in The 'Battle for Berlin'. At a darker remove, the theme extends to the point of the subject creature's extinction ('Thylacine stomp'). Countering these pieces, there is the straightforward, more buoyant and wondrous appreciation of animals evoked in 'Sea eagle' and 'Whippet'. There is the ironic consideration of 'Shark: "Bite" ' (which connects the subject creature to the notion of inadequacies in our human language); and playfulness again in the two crocodile contemplations ('Crocodiles: the Far North', and 'Crocodile: a re-evaluation'), as well as in the evocation of world-weary elephantine despair toward human behaviour depicted in '*The Roots of Heaven*'.

Finally, this broad collection theme extends to human interaction with landscape and natural space: in 'The willow-slayers', and 'Snow gums (The ridge)', and in the two long, 'conjectural' bucolics ('The Darling at Menindee' and 'If Nappa Merrie was the Berkshire Downs'); as well as the bemused touristic pondering in 'The deep freeze'. These pieces contrasting again with the more purely positive appreciation of nature's grace and bounty seen in 'Wildlife', 'Chalk stream', and 'Ducks, Lake Vembanad'. On top of this, there are takes on the more abstract geography of the heavens ('Skyfall'), and on the remote landscape of the moon ('*Eagle* debriefing' again).

* * *

As indicated, some poems here have been shaped over a long period of time. The seed for the title poem sequence was a sonnet published in the *Canberra Times* 15 years ago, back in 2009, and withheld from publication in intervening collections for want of developing the poem through further stanzas—finally completed just in the last few months. For the same period of time I had nursed this collection's title, which is a spin-off from Evelyn Waugh's dark-comedic 1942 novel *Put Out More Flags*—with my amendment intending to supplant the original jingoistic connotation with my own one of benignly heroic (perhaps sometimes brazenly naive?) perseverance shown in face of humankind's and nature's various besiegements, dire and less dire, across multiple fronts in this world. The oldest poems in this collection are '*Eagle* debriefing' and 'Skyfall', first sketched out some 30 years ago, and pulled for a bit of revision following Recent Work Press's invitation to submit to their *Giant Steps* commemorative moonlanding anthology of 2019. 'Apricot drop' was likewise first drafted several decades ago, from my wife's recalling a childhood experience on the northern tablelands of NSW. 'Filial: the detectives' was initially drafted in the mid-1990s, developed from a conversation I had during seven year's residence in Armidale prior to our family's coming to Canberra. The second part of 'Two songs for porcines' relates an event from a university hitchhiking trip in my early 20s. 'The pilot station: a lament' was originally sketched out during a writing residency at Camden Haven in 2017.

At the opposite end of things, some of these poems were both conceived and completed within just the last few recent years. These include 'The tiger quoll coat' (based, perhaps surprisingly, on someone's real, lived experience—though not my own); the two crocodile poems (deriving from a Queensland road trip of mid-2022); and 'Instructions for playing piano'—which was inspired by my wife's surprise gifting me with a Roland keyboard for my 70th birthday just last year (constituting for me a remarkably short—'miraculous,' really—period for genesis and final realisation of a poem). Obviously recent too, with its contemporary political references, is 'Prescription for joy and peace in this world'—which is also quite different in its style, being conceived as a sort of breathless 'mash-up' with something of the energy of an unrhymed 'rap' piece, driven by its relentless, cockamamie, hyper-energised links and rhythm.

Revisiting your earlier drafted work (and self) is an interesting process. On very rare occasions an older poem might actually require relatively little revision, but more likely it requires considerable to massive work in cutting, slashing, and reshaping. (Drafts of a few of the older 'cookpot' poems survive in foolscap, in the imprint of the Olympia 'Monica' portable typewriter my parents gave me for my 21st birthday, fifty years ago—the manuscripts subsequently being carried in my backpack in a nine-month Asia-overland journey to London in 1984-85, then flown back to Australia to be toted through multiple abodes in Sydney, Armidale and finally on to Canberra. They have travelled many obscene thousands of kilometres, at the cost of inexcusable greenhouse emissions. *Mea culpa!*)

The delay in publication of any particular older poem (beyond my failing to discover any valid, worthwhile imaginative 'truth' in it, or its being essentially banal in conception or form) can generally be explained in terms of the ongoing struggle for craft: to find the poem's essential core; the correct 'point of attack' to address its theme; the right 'voice' for freeing the poem up and properly, naturally, energising it; to discover, and then hold, the right tone—get the right rhythms, and 'breath'. Then editing and honing it further by repeatedly reading it, both silently and aloud, until it feels 'right' and 'ripe' in the mouth. Trying to ensure that, whatever its subject or length, the poem in some way hopefully proves 'fresh' and 'interesting'. That it 'engages', and 'entertains' in the best and fullest sense of that word. That it 'stands up' to warrant the reader's/ listener's time and attention, and justify your diverting them from Netflix. (Though of course, even upon publication, chances are you will still not have got everything right; and may even later care to disown it.)

* * *

Regarding poetic themes (interests? obsessions?), I've sometimes been surprised to realise these remain largely unchanged from those I held back in my early 20s and appearing in my first collection, *The Wolf Problem in Australia*—published under Five Islands Press's 'New Poets' program in 1994, exactly 30 years ago this year. Growing older, I've naturally acquired additional experiences (most prominent and impactful among them being marriage and parenting), and I find too that I've developed an even more intense interest in history, and the formative events and experiences of earlier generations. A particular aspect of this is the Second World War, which is a focus for poems here, just as it was in my first and some subsequent intervening collections. As my own generation, which had family members directly involved in the events and sacrifices of that conflict, is being gradually nudged out the door, it feels important to me to help keep that history alive—to memorialise, reimagine, or critique aspects of it. For me this fits under the subheading of 'responsibility' which forms up one of the present collection's themes.

Beyond this, I'd say that the impulse for my writing is born of my broad (sometimes admittedly rather fey or quirky) musing on the world; and musing on the self through the various, cumulative life-stages. As well as being driven by continual delighted delving into the fascinating possibilities of the language, in both formal and vernacular registers. In an essential sense, I consider writing to be 'play' and 'game'. It embraces serendipity; and sometimes you might chance your arm. You can mix it all up: from shorter pieces to longer poems, from more formal and spare or austere styles, to treading the baroque edge of the more 'wild and woolly'. You can be serious with poetry while still sometimes having some fun and occasionally being funny along the way.

Notes

'The oar (*improvisation after Rosemary Dobson's 'The Sailor' 1960*)': There is an interesting discussion on Dobson's poem in an online article posted 2015: 'Too Many Times Adrift'—from 'bypoetlines', who identifies themself as an ex-seaman. 'There was always this standard response ... if you asked [sailors] what they were going to do when they paid off ... "Mate ... I'm going to put an oar on my shoulder and keep walking inland with me back to the sea until somebody says, 'What's that'?"... So [in Dobson's poem] the sailor kept walking until he came across people who had never seen an oar, [and were] therefore not tainted with any of the crap from life at sea, so he knows he can live there and forget his past ...' See: https://bypoetlines.blogspot.com/2015/02/

'The deep freeze': Thanks to Kati Gorgenyi for physical details on Nuuk used here.

'Skyfall': Source, *Mysteries of the Unexplained*, Reader's Digest, 1982

'The Roots of Heaven': A 1958 Hollywood film, based on Romain Gary's novel of the same name. Some relating facts derived from Artemis Cooper's biography: *Patrick Leigh Fermor, an adventure*, 2012. The line, 'It seems that everything beautiful in it is doomed to go' is a slightly amended quote from the original (Sources: Wikipedia and IMDB).

'The pig: a defence': Biblical reference to swine at Gadarenes: Luke 8:26-39

"The Cardinal': The poem presenting the clerical persona here was completed when Cardinal Pell was serving time for charges of sexual abuse against two 13-year-old choirboys, committed in the late 1990s in St Patricks Cathedral, Melbourne—prior to his subsequent appeal. He was sentenced to six years imprisonment in 2019. The jury's guilty verdict was upheld by an appeals court in 2019, but Pell took his case to the High Court of Australia, arguing that the jury's verdict had relied too heavily on evidence of his accuser ('Witness J'). His lawyers didn't try to discredit that earlier testimony, but argued that other evidence had not been properly considered, and that Pell had not been proven guilty beyond reasonable doubt. The High Court agreed, and the verdict was quashed, with Pell subsequently freed in April 2020 after serving 13 months. Over this same period there was widespread public discussion of other alleged behaviour by Pell against boys while serving as a priest in Ballarat, and further instances. (Prosecution of a case relating to allegations of his sexually assaulting two boys while throwing them in the air in a Ballarat swimming pool in the late 1970s had not been proceeded with.) There was likewise criticism of Pell's failure to disclose the acts of paedophile priests, with the Royal Commission into Institutional Responses to Child Sexual Abuse (2020) finding that he had known of such abuse in the 1970s but failed to take adequate action to address it. Pell was also publicly criticised for his perceived support of the paedophile priest offender Gerald Ridsdale, and for his overbearing (perceived 'unempathic') behaviour towards sexual assault victims, their families and supporters. Cardinal Pell persistently maintained his innocence of these and other allegations.

As Australia's highest ranked Catholic cleric, George Pell was first prefect of the Secretariat for the Economy (akin to being Vatican Treasurer), in charge of overseeing Vatican finances from 2014 to 2019—exercising economic control and vigilance over the agencies of the Holy See, including investigating inefficiencies and malpractice in Vatican financial affairs. (Wikipedia and other sources.)

'Thylacine stomp': This poem is based on the longest composite footage (45 seconds, black & white) of the male thylacine allegedly called 'Benjamin'—filmed by David Fleay in December 1933, and believed to have died of keeper's neglect after being locked out of its sheltered sleeping quarters and exposed to a rare occurrence of extreme Tasmanian weather fluctuations. (Coloured/digitised 80 second clip of same produced by National Film & Sound Archive, 2021.) The last actual thylacine footage is of the same animal in the same compound filmed in 1935, in a shorter 21-second sequence tourist promotion, *Tasmania the Wonderland*; probably shot by Sidney Cook. However it has recently been revealed that the actual last-surviving animal was an aged female sold to the zoo by a trapper in May 1936. (The sale was not recorded or publicised because the ground-based snaring he used was illegal.) This thylacine only lived for a few months, and died on 7 September 1936, with its remains being transferred to the Tasmanian Museum and Gallery and lying there undiscovered until a collection audit in 2022. (Source: Wikipedia, and Tasmanian Museum and Art Gallery website.)

'Orison for Oates': It is a scientific postulation that the bodies could indeed have been carried off by the moving ice and deposited in the sea in this way.

'Beechey Island': Poem inspired by the documentary *Buried in Ice* (Beattie, Owen, 1988). The bodies of Franklin Expedition members Petty Officer John Torrington, Royal Marine Private William Braine, and Able Seaman John Hartnell were buried on Beechey Island in 1846. A filmed survey of the graves was undertaken in 1986, shown in an episode of the American television program *Nova*. The team noticed that someone had previously attempted to exhume John Hartnell, a pick axe having damaged his coffin lid. Later research revealed that Sir Edward Belcher, commander of one of the Franklin rescue expeditions, had ordered the exhumation in October 1852 but was thwarted by permafrost. Commander Edward A. Inglefield succeeded a month later, removing the coffin's plaque. Unlike Hartnell's grave, that of Private Braine was largely intact, though showing signs of hasty burial, with one of his undershirts having been put on backwards and the small coffin's lid pressing down on his nose. In 2014, HMS *Erebus* was located in good condition at the bottom of Wilmot and Crampton Bay, in Queen Maud Gulf (*Hunt for the Arctic Ghost Ship*, prod. Lion Television for Channel 4's 'Secret History' series, 2015). In 2016, the Arctic Research Foundation expedition found the wreck of HMS *Terror* in Terror Bay. Cumulative research has determined that the Beechey Island crew probably died of pneumonia, and perhaps tuberculosis. Toxicological reports pointing also to lead poisoning (from soldering in the food cans), though more recent re-examination of bone and nail samples casts doubt on this (additional information Wikipedia).

'*Shoes of the Danube*': Sculpture installation by Can Togay & Gyula Pauer, 2005. Set on Budapest embankment in remembrance of 3500 people, including 800 Jews, executed there by the Arrow Cross militia, 1944–45.

Acknowledgments

Some of these poems (in a different version) have been published previously:

'Wildlife (Dunbogan)', *Wild* anthology (ed Joan Fenney), Ginninderra Press, 2018

'The "Fisher-of-Men" is a "Fisher-of-Women" too', *Canberra Times,* 2018

'*Eagle* lands' and 'Skyfall': *Giant Steps* anthology (ed Shane Strange and Paul Munden), Recent Work Press, 2019

The first section of the 'Put out more prayer flags' sequence, was published as 'Prayer Flags: Made to Fade', in the *Canberra Times,* 2009

'The Fall of Communism (The Russians are Coming)', *I Protest!: Poems of Dissent,* anthology (ed Stephen Matthews), Ginninderra Press, 2020

'Sea eagle (Quaama)': published as 'Eagle's Nest', *The Book of Birds* anthology (ed Penelope Layland & Lesley Lebkowicz), Recent Work Press, 2023

'The pilot station: a lament' is based on the experience of a two-week Writers Residency at the Camden Head Pilot Station (Dunbogan, mid-north coast of NSW) in April 2017. Residencies initiated by the late Eric Rolls and his wife Elaine van Kempen, and conducted in association with the trustees, Camden Haven Community College and volunteers.

Special thanks to Shane Strange and his valiant and wonderful Recent Work Press. Thanks to Dave and Kim Coulton for hospitality and inspiration at Nappa Merrie. And to Ross, and Camden Haven Community College, for the Pilot Station residency.

About the author

Photo: Skye Blomfield

Paul Cliff is a Canberra-based poet, playwright and editor. Among a number of jobs, including early work as a stagehand at the Sydney Opera House, he has principally worked as a book editor, including serving as Senior Editor in the publications sections of the National Library of Australia and the National Gallery of Australia. This is his sixth book of poetry (in addition to three chapbooks). His collection, *A Constellation of Abnormalities*, won the ACT Publishing Award for Poetry in 2018. Among other awards and prizes, he has won the David Campbell Poetry Award, while his experimental play, *Deadline: A Manual for Hostage-Taking*, won the Canberra Playwright's Award 2000 and was produced by Canberra Repertory at Canberra's Theatre 3. He can be heard talking about his approach to writing, and reading sample poems from his published work, which now ranges across a period of 30 years, in an interview conducted for ArtSound FM's 'Poetry on the Radio' series, recorded in Canberra in January 2024.

www.ingramcontent.com/pod-product-compliance
Ingram Content Group Australia Pty Ltd
76 Discovery Rd, Dandenong South VIC 3175, AU
AUHW020639050325
407891AU00002B/6